WELCOME!

On behalf of Splash! Publications, we would like to welcome you to *Westward Expansion*, one of several books in our American History series. Since this curriculum was designed by teachers, we are positive that you will find it to be the most comprehensive program you have ever utilized to teach students about Westward Expansion. We would like to take a few moments to familiarize you with the program.

THE FORMAT

Westward Expansion is a ten lesson program. Our goal is a curriculum that you can use the very first day you purchase our materials. No lessons to plan, comprehension questions to write, activities to create, or vocabulary words to define. Simply open the book and start teaching.

Each of the 10 lessons requires students to complete vocabulary cards, read about a Westward Expansion topic, and complete a Reading comprehension activity that will expose them to various standardized test formats. In addition, each lesson includes a balanced mix of lower and higher level activities for students to complete. Vocabulary quizzes, thought provoking discussion questions about famous people in history, primary and secondary source activities, scale mapping activities, writing and research activities utilizing graphic organizers that include Venn diagrams and K•W•L•H charts, using research to create games, and journaling about the animals of the Pacific Northwest are the types of activities that will guide students through their journey of *Westward Expansion*.

THE LESSON PLANS

On the next several pages, you will find the Lesson Plans for *Westward Expansion*. The Lesson Plans clearly outline what students must do before, during, and after each lesson. Page numbers are listed so that you will immediately know what you need to photocopy before beginning each lesson. The answers to all activities, quizzes, and comprehension questions can be found on pages 132-138.

THE VOCABULARY

Each lesson features words in bold type. We have included a Glossary on pages 125-131 to help students pronounce and define the words. Unlike a dictionary, the definitions in the Glossary are concise and written in context. Remember, we're teachers! Students will be exposed to these vocabulary words in the comprehension activities. They will also be tested on the vocabulary words seven times throughout their study of *Westward Expansion*.

Students will be responsible for filling out and studying the vocabulary cards. You may want to have students bring in a small box for storing their vocabulary cards. We don't have to tell you that incorporating these words into your Reading and Spelling programs will save time and make the words more meaningful for students.

CORE STANDARDS: THE "BIG IDEAS"

Core Standards help teachers prioritize instruction and connect the "big ideas" students need to know in order to advance. As a reading-based unit, *Westward Expansion* fosters literacy in Social Studies.

At the same time that students are learning important factual content about *Westward Expansin*, they are meeting the Common Core Standards for English Language Arts and making connections to the "big ideas" in American History. Alignment to the 3rd-5th Grade Common Core Standards is clearly noted in the Lesson Plans. Below is the legend used to abbreviate the Common Core Strands:

COMMON CORE STRAND CODE:
CC = COMMON CORE
RL = READING-LITERATURE
RI = READING INFORMATIONAL TEXT
RF = READING FOUNDATIONS SKILLS
W = WRITING
SL = SPEAKING LISTENING
L = LANGUAGE

THE COPYRIGHT

Our Other Titles

COMPLETE STATE HISTORY PROGRAMS
Do American History!
Do Arizona!
Do California!
Do Colorado!
Do Florida!
Do Nevada!
Do New Mexico!
Do Texas!
Do Washington!

LITERATURE STUDY GUIDES
Charlotte's Web
Cricket in Times Square
Enormous Egg
Sarah, Plain and Tall

PRIMARY SERIES
Leveled Math: Addition Bk 1
Leveled Math: Addition Bk 2
Leveled Math: Subtraction Bk 1
Leveled Math: Subtraction Bk 2
National Holidays
National Symbols
Poems for Every Holiday
Poems for Every Season

AMERICAN HISTORY SERIES
New World Explorers
Spanish Explorers & Conquistadors
The Thirteen Original Colonies
Early American Government
The American Revolution
Slavery in America
The Civil War

U.S. REGION SERIES
The Middle Atlantic States
The New England States
The Great Lakes States
The Great Plains States
The Southeast States
The Southwest States
The Mountain States
The Pacific States

STATE HISTORY SERIES
Arizona Geography
Arizona Animals
Arizona History
Arizona Government & Economy
California Geography
California Animals
California History
California Government & Economy
Florida Geography
Florida Animals
Florida History
Florida Government & Economy
Illinois History
Indiana History
Michigan History
Ohio History
Texas Geography
Texas Animals
Texas History
Texas Government & Economy

TABLE OF CONTENTS

WESTWARD EXPANSION

TABLE OF CONTENTS

WESTWARD EXPANSION (CONTINUED)

Lessons at a Glance

1. Before reading The New World, students will:
- complete Vocabulary Cards for *allies, autobiography, biographies, boundaries, coast, colonists, debt, defeated, disputed, England, European, expansion, Great Britain, Great Lakes, independence, island, kidnapped, military, missions, mother country, New World, profit, Revolutionary War, surrendered, treaty.* *(pg. 1)*

After reading The New World *(pps. 2-4)*, students will:
- answer The New World Reading Comprehension Questions. *(pg. 5)*
- differentiate between primary and secondary sources. *(pg. 6)*
- take a Vocabulary Quiz for Westward Expansion Part I. *(pps. 7-8)*

THE NEW WORLD LESSON IS ALIGNED WITH THESE 3RD-5TH GRADE CORE STANDARDS:
CC.RI.1, CC.RI.2, CC.RI.3, CC.RI.4, CC.RI.6, CC.RI.7, CC.RI.10, CC.RF.3A, CC.RF.4A, CC.RF.4C, CC.L.4A, CC.L.4C, CC.L.6

2. Before reading The Louisiana Purchase, students will:
- complete Vocabulary Cards for *advised, capital, Caribbean, citizens, Congress, Constitution, contributions, elected, empire, expedition, exported, federal, mansion, navigate, negotiate, plantations, port, ratify, retreat, rumors, surplus, transport, variety.* *(pg. 1)*

After reading The Louisiana Purchase *(pps. 9-12)*, students will:
- answer The Louisiana Purchase Reading Comprehension Questions. *(pg. 13)*
- complete Lewis and Clark K•W•L•H Chart Part I. *(pps. 14-16)*
- take a Vocabulary Quiz for Westward Expansion Part II. *(pps. 17-18)*

THE LOUISIANA PURCHASE LESSON IS ALIGNED WITH THESE 3RD-5TH GRADE CORE STANDARDS:
CC.RI.1, CC.RI.2, CC.RI.3, CC.RI.4, CC.RI.5, CC.RI.6, CC.RI.7, CC.RI.10, CC.RF.3A, CC.RF.4A, CC.RF.4C, CC.W.7, CC.W.8, CC.L.4A, CC.L.4C, CC.L.6

LESSONS AT A GLANCE

3. Before reading The Lewis and Clark Expedition, students will:
- complete Vocabulary Cards for *appendix, astronomer, border, botanist, captive, convince, culture, currents, escorted, frontier, governor, headwaters, historians, hostile, interpreter, keelboat, prairie, priests, regiment, siblings, surveyor, tomahawks, tuberculosis.* (pg. 1)

After reading The Lewis and Clark Expedition *(pps. 19-23)*, students will:
- answer The Lewis and Clark Expedition Reading Comprehension Questions. *(pg. 24)*
- read about Zebulon Pike and answer thought provoking discussion questions. *(pps. 25-28)*
- complete Lewis and Clark K•W•L•H Chart Parts II-IV. *(pps. 29-30)*
- take a Vocabulary Quiz for Westward Expansion Part III. *(pps. 31-32)*

THE LEWIS AND CLARK LESSON IS ALIGNED WITH THESE 3RD-5TH GRADE CORE STANDARDS:
CC.RI.1, CC.RI.2, CC.RI.3, CC.RI.4, CC.RI.5, CC.RI.6, CC.RI.7, CC.RI.10, CC.RF.3A, CC.RF.4A, CC.RF.4C, CC.W.1A, CC.W.1B, CC.W.2A, CC.W.2B, CC.W.2C, CC.W.2D, CC.W.2E, CC.W.4, CC.W.5, CC.W.7, CC.W.8, CC.W.9B, CC.W.10, CC.L.4A, CC.L.4C, CC.L.6

4. Before reading The Santa Fe Trail, students will:
- complete Vocabulary Cards for *addicted, centuries, ceremonies, companions, competition, fertile, Great Plains, illegally, immigrated, infectious, North America, Pacific Northwest, pelts, pioneers, pursuit, Quakers, small pox, tortured, typhoid fever.* (pg. 1)

After reading The Santa Fe Trail *(pps. 33-34)*, students will:
- answer The Santa Fe Trail Reading Comprehension Questions. *(pg. 35)*
- read about Daniel Boone and answer thought provoking discussion questions. *(pps. 36-38)*

THE SANTA FE TRAIL LESSON IS ALIGNED WITH THESE 3RD-5TH GRADE CORE STANDARDS:
CC.RI.1, CC.RI.2, CC.RI.3, CC.RI.4, CC.RI.5, CC.RI.7, CC.RI.10, CC.RF.3A, CC.RF.4A, CC.RF.4C, CC.W.1A, CC.W.1B, CC.W.9B, CC.L.4A, CC.L.4C, CC.L.6

Lessons at a Glance

5. Before reading The Pacific Northwest, students will:
- complete Vocabulary Cards for *ammunition, annual, artifacts, Asia, baleen, barbed, canine, circumvent, climate, conflict, Continental Army, defend, descendants, estuary, fasted, generosity, harbor, harpoon, headquarters, herbivores, hostile, inactive, influence, inhabited, mammals, mountainous, omnivores, peninsula, poverty, predators, preserved, prey, province, recognition, recreation, resources, respect, retiring, ritual, rodents, sand bars, sculptures, shallow, species, talons, tension, tides, voyage, waterfowl.* (pg. 1)

After reading The Pacific Northwest *(pps. 39-42)*, students will:
- answer The Pacific Northwest Reading Comprehension Questions. *(pg. 43)*
- read about the Makah and answer thought provoking discussion questions. *(pps. 44-45)*
- read about Robert Gray and answer thought provoking discussion questions. *(pps. 46-48)*
- create a Pacific Northwest Expert's Journal about the area's mammals and birds. *(pps. 49-68)*
- take a Vocabulary Quiz for Westward Expansion Part IV. *(pps. 69-70)*

THE PACIFIC NORTHWEST LESSON IS ALIGNED WITH THESE 3RD-5TH GRADE CORE STANDARDS:
CC.RI.1, CC.RI.2, CC.RI.3, CC.RI.4, CC.RI.5, CC.RI.7, CC.RI.10, CC.RF.3A, CC.RF.4A, CC.RF.4C, CC.W.1A, CC.W.1B, CC.W.7, CC.W.8, CC.W.9B, CC.L.4A, CC.L.4C, CC.L.6

6. Before reading The Texas Revolution, students will:
- complete Vocabulary Cards for *adobe, adopted, appointed, attorney general, Catholic, chronic, commander, convention, delegate, enforced, execution, financial, harsh, interfere, invaded, loyal, outnumbered, outraged, plantation, promoted, raids, rebelled, republic, resigned, Supreme Court.* (pg. 1)

After reading The Texas Revolution *(pps. 71-74)*, students will:
- answer The Texas Revolution Reading Comprehension Questions. *(pg. 75)*
- read about Andrew Jackson and answer thought provoking discussion questions. *(pps. 76-78)*
- take a Vocabulary Quiz for Westward Expansion Part V. *(pps. 79-80)*

THE TEXAS REVOLUTION LESSON IS ALIGNED WITH THESE 3RD-5TH GRADE CORE STANDARDS:
CC.RI.1, CC.RI.2, CC.RI.3, CC.RI.4, CC.RI.5, CC.RI.10, CC.RF.3A, CC.RF.4A, CC.RF.4C, CC.W.1A, CC.W.1B, CC.W.9B, CC.L.4A, CC.L.4C, CC.L.6

LESSONS AT A GLANCE

7. Before reading The Oregon Trail, students will:
- complete Vocabulary Cards for *acquired, Continental Divide, Christianity, devoted, discrimination, epidemic, exclusion, founded, gristmill, legislature, merchant, missionaries, Mormon, reservation, sawmill, servants, Sierra Nevada, veteran.* *(pg. 1)*

After reading The Oregon Trail *(pps. 81-84)*, students will:
- answer The Oregon Trail Reading Comprehension Questions. *(pg. 85)*
- read about George Washington Bush and answer thought provoking discussion questions. *(pps. 86-88)*

THE OREGON TRAIL LESSON IS ALIGNED WITH THESE 3RD-5TH GRADE CORE STANDARDS:
CC.RI.1, CC.RI.2, CC.RI.3, CC.RI.4, CC.RI.5, CC.RI.7, CC.RI.10, CC.RF.3A, CC.RF.4A, CC.RF.4C, CC.W.1A, CC.W.1B, CC.W.9B, CC.L.4A, CC.L.4C, CC.L.6

8. Before reading The Mexican War, students will:
- complete Vocabulary Cards for *basin, Civil War, contrast, estate, formation, inland, repossessed, senator, superior, Union Army.* *(pg. 1)*

After reading The Mexican War *(pps. 89-90)*, students will:
- answer The Mexican War Reading Comprehension Questions. *(pg. 91)*
- read about John C. Frémont and Kit Carson and create a Venn Diagram comparing and contrasting the two pathfinders. *(pps. 92-95)*
- write a paragraph comparing and contrasting Frémont and Carson. *(pg. 96)*
- take a Vocabulary Quiz for Western Expansion Part VI. *(pps. 97-98)*

THE MEXICAN WAR LESSON IS ALIGNED WITH THESE 3RD-5TH GRADE CORE STANDARDS:
CC.RI.1, CC.RI.2, CC.RI.3, CC.RI.4, CC.RI.5, CC.RI.7, CC.RI.10, CC.RF.3A, CC.RF.4A, CC.RF.4C, CC.W.2A, CC.W.2B, CC.W.2C, CC.W.2D, CC.W.2E, CC.W.4, CC.W.5, CC.W.7, CC.W.8, CC.W.9B, CC.W.10, CC.L.4A, CC.L.4C, CC.L.6

Lessons at a Glance

9. Before reading The Gold Rush, students will:
- complete Vocabulary Cards for *admired, blacksmith, carpenter, Confederate Army, construction, customs, donation, former, prospectors, sacred, shafts, threatened, tributaries. (pg. 1)*

After reading The Gold Rush *(pps. 99-103)*, students will:
- answer The Gold Rush Reading Comprehension Questions. *(pg. 104)*
- read about George Custer and Sitting Bull and create the game Find the Fib. *(pps. 105-110)*
  Note: You will need to make four copies of page 109 or 110 for students.

THE GOLD RUSH LESSON IS ALIGNED WITH THESE 3RD-5TH GRADE CORE STANDARDS:
CC.RI.1, CC.RI.2, CC.RI.3, CC.RI.4, CC.RI.7, CC.RI.10, CC.RF.3A, CC.RF.4A, CC.RF.4C, CC.W.7, CC.W.8, CC.L.4A, CC.L.4C, CC.L.6

10. Before reading Westward Transportation, students will:
- complete Vocabulary Cards for *gliders, granite, inventor, manufactured, monument, public transportation, quarry, steamboat, telegraph, transcontinental, vessel. (pg. 1)*

After reading Westward Transportation *(pps. 111-116)*, students will:
- answer Westward Transportation Reading Comprehension Questions. *(pg. 117)*
- use a scale ruler to measure the distance traveled by the Pony Express. *(pps. 118-121)*
- construct a Pony Express map showing the famous route. *(pg. 122)*
- take a Vocabulary Quiz for Western Expansion Part VII. *(pps. 123-124)*

THE GOLD RUSH LESSON IS ALIGNED WITH THESE 3RD-5TH GRADE CORE STANDARDS:
CC.RI.1, CC.RI.2, CC.RI.3, CC.RI.4, CC.RI.7, CC.RI.10, CC.RF.3A, CC.RF.4A, CC.RF.4C, CC.L.4A, CC.L.4C, CC.L.6

Vocabulary Card

word: _____

definition: _____

_____

Vocabulary Card

word: _____

definition: _____

_____

Vocabulary Card

word: _____

definition: _____

_____

THE NEW WORLD

The United States is a large area of land divided into 50 states. You probably know that a little more than 200 years ago, the United States contained just 13 states crowded along the Atlantic **Coast**. Have you ever wondered how and when the 37 other states were added? Studying about the history of the United States and Westward **Expansion** will help you answer this and many other questions.

ENGLISH COLONIES

In 1585, English **colonists** from the **Island** of **Great Britain** sailed across the Atlantic Ocean and claimed land in what they called the **New World**. Although the first two colonies failed, **England** made plans to try again. Less than 150 years later, England had successfully established 13 colonies along the Atlantic Coast of America.

FRENCH AND SPANISH COLONIES

Of course, England wasn't the only country claiming land in the New World. By the time England's 13 colonies were established, France had claimed Canada, the Mississippi River Valley, and most of the land in the **Great Lakes** region.

Spain had taken control of Florida and most of the land west of the Mississippi River.

SPANISH MISSIONS

Each country built permanent settlements guarded by soldiers for protection. West of the Mississippi River, Spain built **missions**. Spanish soldiers **kidnapped** Native Americans and forced them to live and work at the missions. The Spanish government hoped that a trained army of Native American soldiers would help if Spain was ever attacked by another country.

BEAVER FURS

East of the Mississippi River, French and English colonists built **military** forts and established trade relationships with the Native Americans. In exchange for beaver furs, the colonists gave the Native Americans metal tools, weapons, and other **European** items the Native Americans had never seen before.

Native Americans in the Great Lakes area trapped beaver and traded with the French colonists. Native Americans who lived along the Atlantic Ocean trapped and traded with the English colonists.

Beaver furs were worth a lot of money to the French and English colonists. The smooth, waterproof beaver furs were shipped back to France and England where they were sold for a very high **profit**. Everyone in France and England wanted a beautiful hat or coat made of beaver fur. The French and English colonists would do anything to protect this business.

THE FRENCH AND INDIAN WAR

The French and English colonists battled for more than 70 years over the control of land and hunting territories. The French and Indian War was the last battle fought between these two countries and their Native American **allies**. Spain allied with France. Great Britain sent soldiers and money to help the English colonists win the war.

When the French and Indian war ended in 1763, France and its allies had been **defeated**. A **treaty** was signed by Great Britain, France, and Spain.

France gave all of its land east of the Mississippi River, except for the city of New Orleans, to Great Britain. Great Britain also received most of France's land in Canada.

Control of the five Great Lakes and all of the valuable hunting territories now belonged to Great Britain. The treaty also required Spain to give its territory in Florida to Great Britain. In return for helping them during the war, France gave its territory west of the Mississippi River and the city of New Orleans, to Spain. The French and Indian War was finally over.

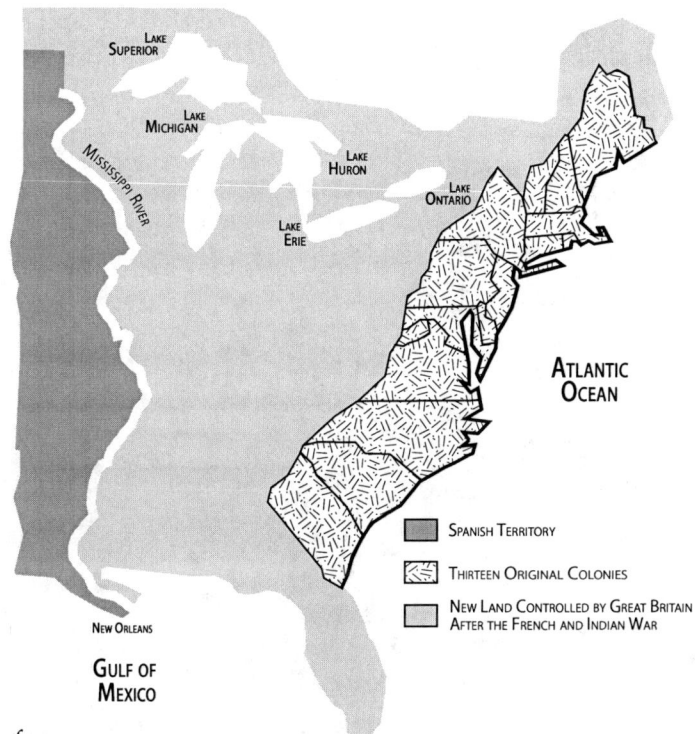

THE REVOLUTIONARY WAR

As soon as the last shots of the French and Indian War were fired, another battle began brewing. This time it was between the English colonists and their **mother country**, Great Britain. It seemed that Great Britain expected the colonists to pay for its help during the French and Indian War. Sending British soldiers and money to help win the war had been very expensive. Great Britain taxed the colonists to pay for the **debt**. Each time the colonists bought paper, stamps, tea, and other British items, they were charged extra money. The additional money was sent to Great Britain to pay the debt created by the war.

The colonists grew tired of Great Britain's control and taxes. In 1775, the first shots of the **Revolutionary War** were fired. The following year, the colonists declared their **independence** from Great Britain and formed the United States of America. The Declaration of Independence did not end the Revolutionary War, but the colonists made it clear to Great Britain that they were willing to fight for their freedom.

In 1781, the Revolutionary War ended. Great Britain **surrendered** to the United States. A treaty was signed recognizing the United States as an independent nation. It was agreed that all land west to the Mississippi River, north to Canada, east to the Atlantic Ocean, and south to Georgia belonged to the United States. The territory of Florida was given back to Spain. As you can see by the map below, the United States had a long way to go before its **boundaries** would be complete.

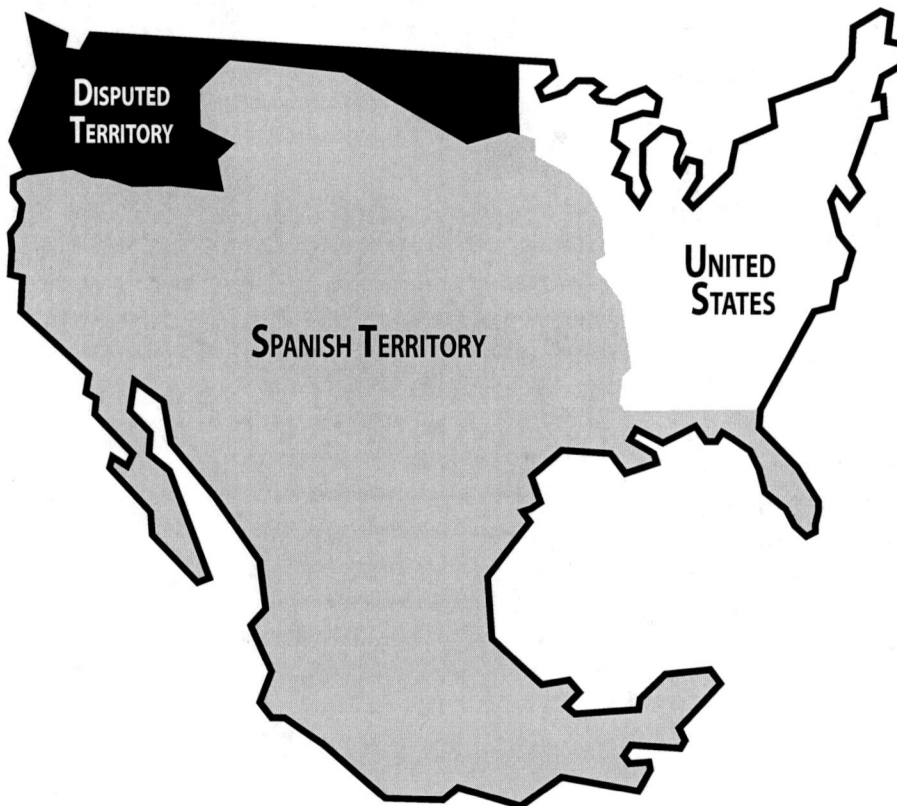

DISPUTED TERRITORY

SPANISH TERRITORY

UNITED STATES

❖❖❖❖❖ THE NEW WORLD ❖❖❖❖❖

Directions: Read each question carefully. Darken the circle for the correct answer.

---

1 How many states are in the United States?

   A 52

   B 13

   C 50

   D 37

2 What can you learn by studying the map of English, French, and Spanish colonies?

   F The English colonies were south of the Gulf of Mexico.

   G The Spanish colonies were south of the French colonies.

   H There were no colonies west of the Atlantic Ocean.

   J The French colonies were east of the English colonies.

3 Which country built missions for protection and kidnapped Native Americans?

   A Spain

   B England

   C Great Britain

   D France

4 After reading about beaver furs, you get the idea that –

   F Spain controlled most of the beaver hunting territories

   G Native Americans were not interested in participating in the fur trade

   H beaver furs were very popular in France and England

   J very little money was made trapping and trading beaver furs

5 The French and Indian War was fought for –

   A control over the beaver hunting territories

   B control of the Spanish missions

   C control of the Mississippi River

   D control over Great Britain's soldiers

6 According to the French and Indian War map, which country took control of Florida after the war?

   F Spain

   G Great Britain

   H France

   J The United States

7 Which country took control of Florida after the Revolutionary War?

   A Spain

   B Great Britain

   C France

   D The United States

READING

Answers

1 Ⓐ Ⓑ Ⓒ Ⓓ   5 Ⓐ Ⓑ Ⓒ Ⓓ

2 Ⓕ Ⓖ Ⓗ Ⓙ   6 Ⓕ Ⓖ Ⓗ Ⓙ

3 Ⓐ Ⓑ Ⓒ Ⓓ   7 Ⓐ Ⓑ Ⓒ Ⓓ

4 Ⓕ Ⓖ Ⓗ Ⓙ

consider
the source

Think about the ways we learn about history. Reading books, seeing movies, looking at photographs, studying maps, searching the Internet, digging for bones, and holding pieces of pottery are some of the ways that we learn about the past.

There are two types of sources to help us learn about what happened in the past. Primary sources are recorded by people who were there at the time. If you have ever read a diary or an **autobiography**, then you were reading something that was written by the person who was actually recording the events and experiences as they were happening. Diaries and autobiographies are primary sources. Letters, interviews, photographs, maps, bones, and pieces of pottery are other examples of primary sources because they give us "first-hand" knowledge of an event that took place in history.

Secondary sources are recorded by people after an event took place. Many books have been written about important historical events and people. A book written in 2005 about the first missionaries in Arizona is a secondary source because the author didn't interview any of the missionaries and can't give any "first-hand" knowledge of their experiences. Movies, **biographies**, newspaper stories, and encyclopedias are other examples of secondary sources because they give us "second-hand" knowledge of events that took place in history.

You have just finished reading about the New World and the countries who once claimed parts of the present-day United States.

In this activity, you will decide whether a source of information is a primary source or a secondary source. On the lines provided, put a "P" next to the primary sources and an "S" next to the secondary sources.

1. _____ A bottle of water scooped from one of the five Great Lakes in 1761.

2. _____ A model of a Spanish mission built by a student in your class.

3. _____ Your great great grandfather's hat made of beaver fur.

4. _____ An encyclopedia article about the French and Indian War.

5. _____ The diary of an English colonist describing his part in the Revolutionary War.

6. _____ The original signatures on the Declaration of Independence.

7. _____ A photograph of a British soldier taken in 1776.

Name _____

꧁꧂ VOCABULARY QUIZ ꧁꧂
WESTWARD EXPANSION
PART I

DIRECTIONS: Match the vocabulary word on the left with its definition on the right. Put the letter for the definition on the blank next to the vocabulary word it matches. Use each word and definition only once.

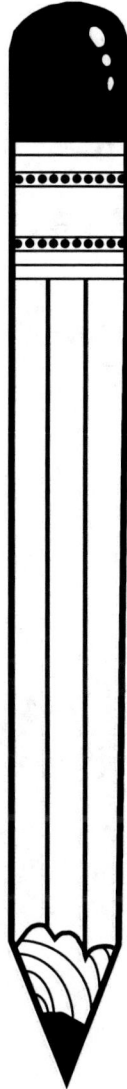

1. _____ treaty

2. _____ allies

3. _____ boundaries

4. _____ surrendered

5. _____ autobiography

6. _____ missions

7. _____ biographies

8. _____ profit

9. _____ Great Lakes

10. _____ coast

11. _____ New World

12. _____ colonists

13. _____ mother country

14. _____ debt

15. _____ Revolutionary War

A. money that is owed to someone else.

B. types of churches.

C. a person who comes from the continent of Europe, the sixth smallest of Earth's seven continents.

D. a formal agreement.

E. took someone without permission.

F. a term used to describe the original homeland of the English colonists.

G. groups of people who come together to help one another in times of trouble.

H. not under the control or rule of someone else.

I. a term once used to describe the continents of North America and South America.

J. won victory over.

K. the process of growing larger.

L. area of land that is completely surrounded by water.

M. the story of your life written by you.

Westward Expansion © 2009
splashpublications.com

7

16. _____ defeated

17. _____ Great Britain

18. _____ disputed

19. _____ kidnapped

20. _____ England

21. _____ island

22. _____ European

23. _____ independence

24. _____ expansion

25. _____ military

N. people who are ruled by another country.

O. an island which includes England, Scotland, and Wales.

P. stories of a person's life written by someone else.

Q. gave up.

R. an area of land that borders water.

S. people who are part of the armed forces who may be asked to go to war.

T. an area that two or more parties disagree about.

U. money made after all expenses have been paid.

V. five large lakes located in North America at the border between Canada and the United States. The names of the lakes are Superior, Michigan, Huron, Erie, and Ontario.

W. a region located on the southern part of the island of Great Britain.

X. battle for independence between the English colonists in America and Great Britain.

Y. dividing lines.

$ THE LOUISIANA PURCHASE

In 1801, Thomas Jefferson became the third president of the United States. Our country was still very young. It had only been 25 years since the 13 original colonies signed the Declaration of Independence and formed the United States of America.

During its first 25 years as a nation, the United States worked hard to form a fair system of government and a strong military. **Citizens** were taxed to pay for everything that a new country with 13 states needed. The United States **Constitution** was written. The Constitution outlined the way **federal** and state governments would be run. The Bill of Rights was written, guaranteeing certain rights and freedoms to every citizen of the United States. Two presidents, George Washington and John Adams had already been **elected**. The nation's **capital** had been moved from New York City to Washington, D.C. The White House had been built and President Jefferson was living and working in the **mansion**.

OUR COUNTRY'S NEIGHBORS

During our country's first 25 years, the boundaries of the United States were much different than what is shown on a map today. The Mississippi River formed the western boundary of the United States. To the west of the United States was the Louisiana Territory. Remember, after losing the French and Indian War, France gave its territory in Louisiana to Spain. This included the city of New Orleans, a very important shipping **port** to the Gulf of Mexico. To the south of the United States was Florida, also controlled by Spain.

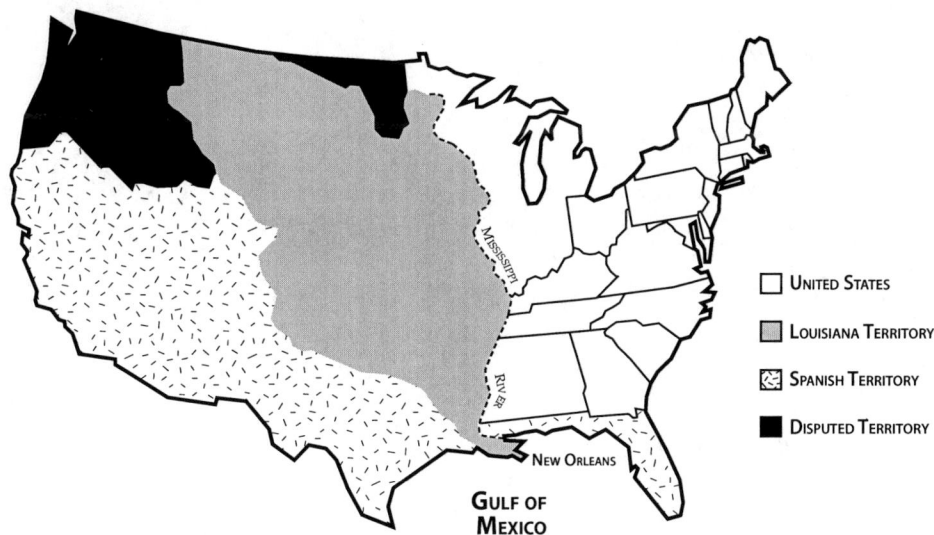

☐ UNITED STATES
▨ LOUISIANA TERRITORY
▨ SPANISH TERRITORY
■ DISPUTED TERRITORY

THE MISSISSIPPI RIVER

The Mississippi River was a very important waterway for the United States. It was used by farmers to **transport** crops to cities along the river. The Mississippi River was also an important route to the Gulf of Mexico. The United States sent **surplus** crops and other American goods down the Mississippi River to the Gulf of Mexico. From the Gulf of Mexico, these items were **exported** to other countries. New Orleans was the last city on the way to the Gulf of Mexico. This city, like the rest of the Louisiana Territory, was controlled by Spain.

In 1795, the United States and Spain signed a treaty. Spain gave the United States permission to **navigate** the entire Mississippi River and use the city of New Orleans to store crops and other items until they were ready to be exported.

Without this permission from Spain, the United States would not be able to export a **variety** of products that included flour, tobacco, pork, butter, cheese, and animal skins.

By 1802, farmers, businessmen, trappers, and lumbermen were exporting more than one million dollars worth of goods from New Orleans to other countries.

THOMAS JEFFERSON

FEAR OF FRANCE

Soon after becoming president, Thomas Jefferson learned that Spain had returned the Louisiana Territory to France. There were **rumors** that Spain also planned to give Florida and its other colonies in America to France. This news worried President Jefferson and the farmers who depended on the Mississippi River. If France took control of the city of New Orleans, the United States would be cut off from the Gulf of Mexico.

On October 18, 1802, the Spanish government closed the city of New Orleans. The United States was no longer permitted to use this city to get to the Gulf of Mexico. President Jefferson had to stop France from gaining control of Spain's other colonies in America. Thomas Jefferson knew that there were only two ways to take action. The United States could declare war and fight for the land, or it could purchase the land from France.

FRANCE'S GRAND PLAN

Napoleon Bonaparte was a very powerful man in France. He was a military and government leader who wanted to create a French **empire** in America. Bonaparte planned to operate his empire from the **Caribbean** island of Santo Domingo where sugar was grown on huge **plantations**.

Exporting sugar to other countries would make France a very rich country.

After taking the Louisiana Territory back from Spain, Napoleon Bonaparte planned to use the land around the Mississippi River to grow crops and raise animals to feed his colony in Santo Domingo. The Mississippi River would be used to transport flour, salt, lumber, and food to France's sugar islands in Santo Domingo.

In 1801, Napoleon Bonaparte put his plan into action. He sent a large military force to take complete control of Santo Domingo.

During the next 10 months, Bonaparte lost over 40,000 soldiers on Santo Domingo to war and yellow fever. He was forced to **retreat** from the island and give up his dreams of creating a French empire in America. Without the profitable sugar trade in Santo Domingo, the Louisiana Territory and the Mississippi River were useless to France.

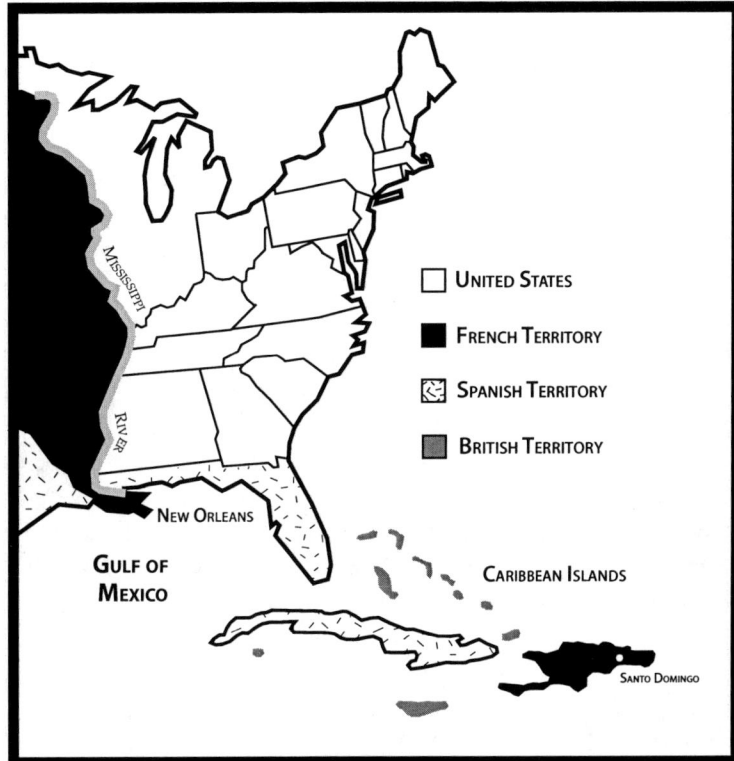

LIVINGSTON AND MONROE

While Napoleon Bonaparte was waging war on the island of Santo Domingo, President Jefferson made plans to purchase the city of New Orleans and part of the Mississippi River.

President Jefferson sent Robert R. Livingston and James Monroe to France. **Congress** allowed the pair to spend no more than two million dollars for the purchase. President Jefferson secretly **advised** Livingston and Monroe to offer France as much as 10 million dollars for Florida and New Orleans. If France wouldn't sell its land, Livingston and Monroe hoped to **negotiate** (neh•GOH•she•ate) a treaty allowing the United States to use New Orleans.

THE LOUISIANA PURCHASE

On April 11, 1803, Robert Livingston and James Monroe arrived in France. They were amazed to learn that Napoleon Bonaparte was offering to sell the entire Louisiana Territory to the United States. The 885,000 square miles of land would cost the United States 15 million dollars, or about four cents per acre.

Livingston and Monroe had not gotten permission to spend 15 million dollars. Since there were no phones or private jets, it would take months to sail back to the United States. They feared that if they waited to hear from President Jefferson, Napoleon Bonaparte might change his mind. On April 30, 1803, Livingston and Monroe agreed to purchase the entire Louisiana Territory for 15 million dollars.

When news of the purchase reached the United States, President Jefferson was surprised. He planned to spend 10 million dollars for the port city of New Orleans. Instead, he received a land package that doubled the size of the United States.

President Jefferson asked Congress to approve the sale. Many of the men in Congress were against the purchase. They felt that the Louisiana Territory was a worthless desert. Still, enough men in Congress voted to **ratify** the Louisiana Purchase. The money to pay for the purchase was borrowed from English and Dutch banks. On December 20, 1803, the United States officially took possession of the Louisiana Territory.

The Louisiana Purchase was one of Thomas Jefferson's greatest **contributions** to the United States. Doubling the size of the United States without losing any American lives paved the way for purchasing other territory. As you will soon learn, the Louisiana Purchase also opened the way for Americans to travel West. It wouldn't take long for the United States to grow and become the most powerful nation in the world.

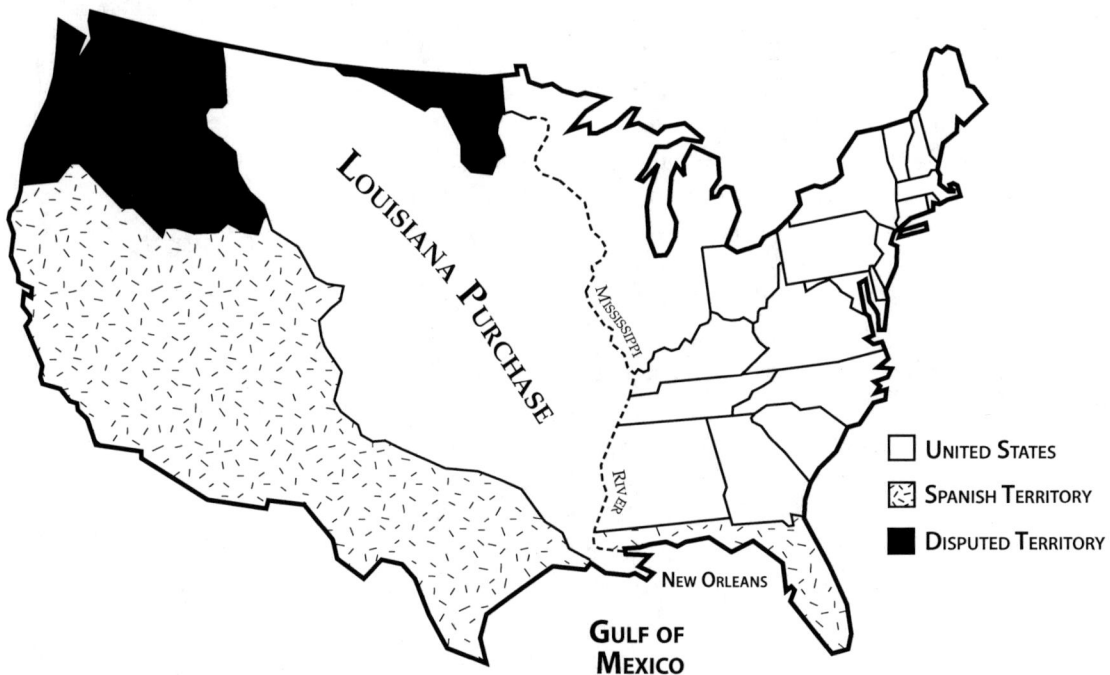

LOUISIANA PURCHASE

Mississippi

River

New Orleans

GULF OF MEXICO

☐ UNITED STATES
▨ SPANISH TERRITORY
■ DISPUTED TERRITORY

Part I

Directions:

1. Use the "What I Know" column of the charts on the next two pages to list facts that you already know about the Lewis and Clark Expedition.

2. Use the "What I Want to Know" column of the charts to list five questions that you have about the Lewis and Clark Expedition. **STOP!** You will fill in the rest of the chart later.

WHAT I KNOW	WHAT I WANT TO KNOW	WHAT I LEARNED	HOW I FOUND OUT	P/S

P / S			
HOW I FOUND OUT			
WHAT I LEARNED			
WHAT I WANT TO KNOW			
WHAT I KNOW			

✦✦✦✦✦✦ VOCABULARY QUIZ ✦✦✦✦✦✦

WESTWARD EXPANSION
PART II

DIRECTIONS: Match the vocabulary word on the left with its definition on the right. Put the letter for the definition on the blank next to the vocabulary word it matches. Use each word and definition only once.

1. _____ advised

2. _____ variety

3. _____ transport

4. _____ surplus

5. _____ capital

6. _____ Caribbean

7. _____ citizens

8. _____ rumors

9. _____ Congress

10. _____ retreat

11. _____ Constitution

12. _____ ratify

13. _____ port

14. _____ contributions

A. the group of men and women in Washington, D.C. who are elected to make laws for the United States.

B. discuss in order to settle something.

C. selected by voting.

D. to give legal approval by voting.

E. sold goods to other countries.

F. an arm of the Atlantic Ocean surrounded on the north and east by the West Indies, on the south by South America, and on the west by Central America.

G. a group of territories or peoples under one ruler.

H. the plan for the United States that outlines the duties of government and guarantees the rights of the people.

I. city or town located next to water with an area for loading and unloading ships.

J. very large farms in the South where crops of cotton and tobacco were grown and slave labor was usually used.

K. a journey for the purpose of exploring.

15. _____ elected

16. _____ plantations

17. _____ empire

18. _____ negotiate

19. _____ expedition

20. _____ navigate

21. _____ exported

22. _____ mansion

23. _____ federal

L.   to back away.

M.   people in a city, town, state, or country who enjoy the freedom to vote and participate in government decisions.

N.   huge home.

O.   helped make a decision and gave advice.

P.   an amount left over.

Q.   acts that involve giving money or time for a special cause.

R.   to move products or people from one place to another.

S.   control the direction of a ship.

T.   government at the national level.

U.   many different kinds.

V.   things said in secret that may or may not be true.

W.   the city that serves as the center of government for the state or nation.

THE LEWIS AND CLARK EXPEDITION

In 1802, almost a full year before the United States purchased the Louisiana Territory, President Thomas Jefferson made plans to explore the unknown land west of the United States. He had heard that the British in Canada had a profitable fur trading business with the Native Americans along the northern **border** of the United States and into the West.

President Jefferson asked Congress to approve an expedition to explore, trade with the Native Americans, and make maps of the area. The president told Congress that he needed $2,500 and a small group of men for the journey.

United States Army officers Meriwether Lewis and William Clark were chosen to lead the expedition. They were expected to bring back information about the land, plants, animals, and the Native Americans. More importantly, President Jefferson hoped that Lewis and Clark would return with news about a water route that connected the Mississippi River to the Pacific Ocean.

PREPARING FOR THE JOURNEY

The journey West would be dangerous. The expedition would pass through Spanish territory with thousands of **hostile** Native Americans.

During the year before the expedition, Lewis and Clark traveled to present-day West Virginia to purchase rifles, knives, **tomahawks**, and other weapons from West Virginia's military stores. They also traveled

LEWIS AND CLARK

to Philadelphia to buy medicine, tents, tools, kettles, tobacco, gunpowder, and gifts for the Native Americans they planned to meet along their journey. In addition, Meriwether Lewis spent time with an **astronomer**, a **botanist**, a **surveyor**, and a doctor. The team needed to be completely prepared for everything they might see during the expedition.

TRAINING FOR THE EXPEDITION

On July 3, 1803, news reached Washington, D. C. that Robert Livingston and James Monroe had just purchased the Louisiana Territory from France. Traveling through land that belonged to the United States would make the journey a bit less dangerous for Lewis and Clark.

More than 50 skilled woodsmen, soldiers, and hunters volunteered to join Lewis and Clark on the expedition. Before leaving on their journey, Lewis and Clark spent the winter training their men.

A spot along the Missouri River was chosen to set up a training camp. It was named Camp River Dubois (doo•BWAH). The men built a road from the mouth of the river through the forest to a nearby **prairie**. Temporary houses were built in the clearing.

During their training, the men hunted wild turkeys and gathered roots. They were expected to keep the camp clean and care for their equipment and clothing. They practiced target shooting and learned how to survive in the wilderness. The men learned about the area they were going to explore from fur traders who had explored the territory before them.

Lewis and Clark planned to travel up the Missouri River in a **keelboat** and two cedar canoes. The keelboat would carry the explorers, while the canoes would carry the food, medicine, scientific instruments, weapons, and gifts for the Native Americans.

FAST FACTS

- Many men volunteered to join Lewis and Clark on their expedition. Only the best volunteers were chosen for the journey. The men who were chosen became part of the United States Army and were paid by the United States government.
- Most of the volunteers had never met each other before. The youngest volunteer was 17 year old George Shannon. The oldest was 35 year old John Shields.

EXPLORING THE WEST

On May 14, 1804, the 8,000-mile expedition left from St. Louis, Missouri. The journey would take more than two years. The group included 45 men, a French **interpreter**, and Captain Lewis's dog.

Traveling up the Missouri River was difficult and exhausting. Extreme heat, injuries, insects, and strong river **currents** made this part of the journey very unpleasant. Lewis's 55-foot long keelboat carried the men, while two smaller boats held all of the supplies. The expedition traveled just 10 to 15 miles each day.

By October, the expedition reached the villages of the Mandan tribe in present-day North Dakota. They built Fort Mandan and spent the winter with the Mandan people.

The villages of the Mandan and their neighbors the Hidatsa (hee•DOT•sah) were the center of a huge trade network in the West. During their stay, Lewis and Clark took careful notes in their journals, drew maps, and hunted buffalo. The weather was very harsh, with temperatures dropping to 40 degrees below zero.

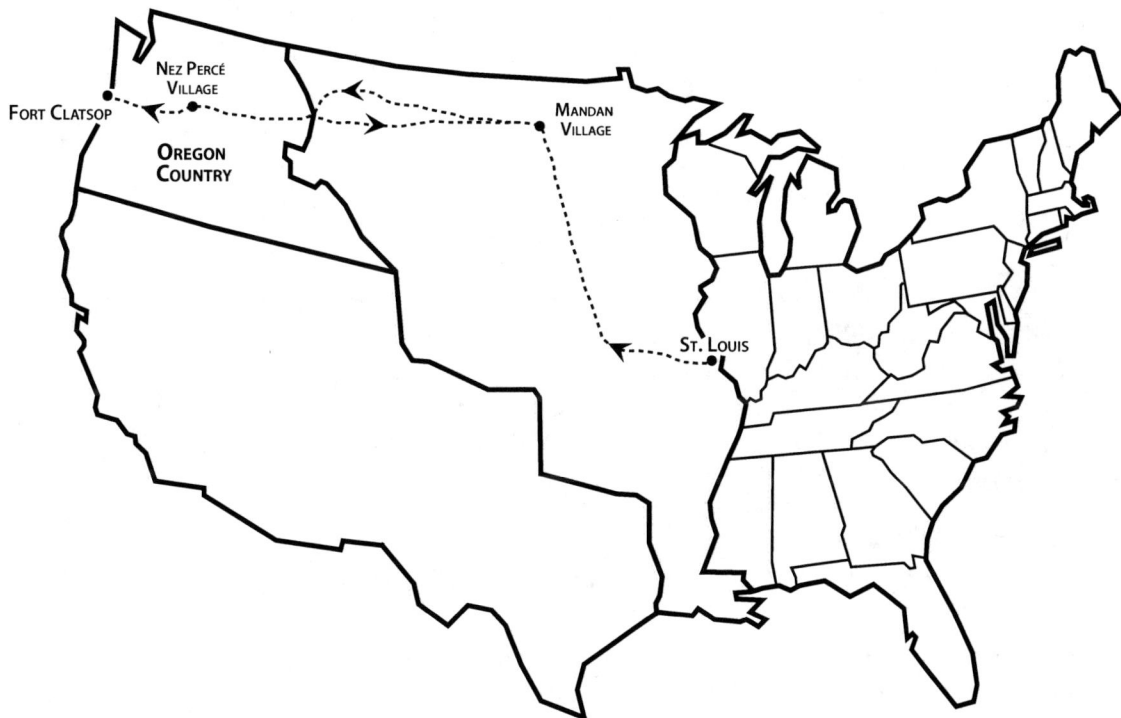

SACAJAWEA (SAK•UH•JUH•WEE•UH)

While staying in the Mandan village, Lewis and Clark met a French fur trader named Toussaint (too•SAHNT) Charbonneau (CAR•bah•no). They hired Charbonneau as an interpreter. Charbonneau agreed to join the expedition as long as he could bring his wife, Sacajawea.

Sacajawea was a Shoshone (show•SHOW•nee) girl. She had been kidnapped by Hidatsa warriors and taken away from her family in the Rocky Mountains when she was just 12 years old. The Hidatsa sold Sacajawea as a slave to the Mandan tribe. Toussaint Charbonneau purchased Sacajawea from the Mandan tribe and married her.

Lewis and Clark agreed to take Sacajawea with them. She could be the group's interpreter if they came in contact with other Native Americans. Sacajawea was only 15 and pregnant when she joined the expedition. She gave birth to a son while on the trip.

In August 1805, the explorers met a band of Shoshone people. Amazingly, Sacajawea learned that the chief of the tribe was her brother. Sacajawea's brother sold horses to the explorers. The horses helped the group cross the dangerous Rocky Mountains.

THE NEZ PERCÉ (NAY•PAIR•SAY)

The most difficult part of the journey came while crossing the Bitterroot Range in the present-day states of Montana and Idaho. The travelers almost starved to death along the Lolo Trail before stumbling into the camp of the Nez Percé tribe.

The Nez Percé had never seen white men before. They could have easily killed the weakened explorers and taken their horses, guns, and supplies. These items would have made the Nez Percé rich and powerful. Instead, the Nez Percé treated the explorers with kindness. The tribe helped them build boats and pointed them in the direction of the Pacific Ocean.

SACAJAWEA

THE PACIFIC OCEAN

In November 1805, the Lewis and Clark expedition reached the Pacific Ocean at the mouth of the Columbia River. To fur traders and explorers, this area was known as Oregon Country. The group hoped to meet a ship that would take them back home. When none appeared, the entire party voted to build a small shelter and wait for warmer weather. The group built Fort Clatsop on the south side of the Columbia River and settled in for the cold, rainy winter.

RETURNING HOME

The next spring, the explorers began the long trip home. They traveled up the Columbia River against strong currents and powerful waterfalls. They waited in the Nez Percé village for the deep mountain snows to melt before crossing the Bitterroot Mountains.

On September 23, 1806, the Lewis and Clark Expedition returned safely to St. Louis. The entire town lined the riverbank to welcome them back. Most were amazed to see the explorers return. They thought that the group had gotten lost or killed by wild animals and Native Americans.

A SUCCESSFUL EXPEDITION

The Lewis and Clark Expedition was declared a success. The biggest disappointment to President Jefferson was that the water route he had hoped for did not exist. The Mississippi River was not connected to the Pacific Ocean. Still, the group had made detailed maps of the area. They had seen beautiful land, rugged mountains, and plenty of wildlife. They brought back important details about the land and the Native Americans. Lewis and Clark even sent a live prairie dog and bones from a forty-five foot dinosaur back to President Jefferson.

Most importantly, the expedition gave the United States a stronger claim to Oregon Country and the present-day states of Idaho, Oregon, and Washington. News of fur bearing animals made Americans want to travel West to explore, trap, and trade with the Native Americans.

FAST FACTS

- Many people suffered from illnesses and injuries during the Lewis and Clark Expedition. Accidental ax and knife cuts, injured shoulders, mosquito bites, and stomach aches from eating strange food were some of the common complaints.
- Everyone survived the journey with Lewis and Clark except Sergeant Charles Floyd. He died after his **appendix** burst.
- The Lewis and Clark Expedition was paid for by the United States government. Most of the people on the journey were in the United States Army. William Clark's black slave, whose name was York, made the entire trip without receiving any pay.

◈◈◈ THE LEWIS AND CLARK EXPEDITION ◈◈◈

Directions: Read each question carefully. Darken the circle for the correct answer.

---

1 President Jefferson wanted Lewis and Clark to explore the West for all of the following reasons <u>except</u> –

  A to bring back Native Americans

  B to find a water route connecting the Mississippi River to the Pacific Ocean

  C to make maps of the area

  D to bring back information about the land, plants, and animals

2 Before making the journey, Meriwether Lewis spent time with a botanist. A <u>botanist</u> is a scientist who studies –

  F animals

  G people

  H plants

  J insects

3 Where did Lewis and Clark train their men before beginning their expedition?

  A The Mississippi River

  B The Gulf of Mexico

  C The Atlantic Ocean

  D The Missouri River

4 Where did the Lewis and Clark Expedition spend its first winter?

  F St. Louis

  G North Dakota

  H Oregon Country

  J Fort Clatsop

5 What can you learn by studying the map of the Lewis and Clark Expedition?

  A The journey started in Oregon Country.

  B The Mandan village was east of the Nez Percé village.

  C The journey headed south from St. Louis.

  D The Mandan village was in Oregon Country.

6 After reading about Sacajawea, you get the idea that –

  F she did not want to join the expedition

  G she was the oldest person on the trip

  H she turned out to be a very valuable part of the expedition

  J Lewis and Clark refused to take her on the expedition

7 Which statement about the Lewis and Clark Expedition is <u>false</u>?

  A Lewis and Clark brought back dinosaur bones.

  B The expedition gave the United States a stronger claim to Oregon Country.

  C President Jefferson was pleased to learn that the Mississippi River was connected to the Pacific Ocean.

  D Lewis and Clark made detailed maps of the area that they explored.

READING

Answers

1 Ⓐ Ⓑ Ⓒ Ⓓ   5 Ⓐ Ⓑ Ⓒ Ⓓ
2 Ⓕ Ⓖ Ⓗ Ⓙ   6 Ⓕ Ⓖ Ⓗ Ⓙ
3 Ⓐ Ⓑ Ⓒ Ⓓ   7 Ⓐ Ⓑ Ⓒ Ⓓ
4 Ⓕ Ⓖ Ⓗ Ⓙ

FAMOUS PEOPLE: ZEBULON MONTGOMERY PIKE

Zebulon Montgomery Pike was born on January 5, 1779. He was the second oldest of eight children. Four of Zebulon's **siblings** died as infants. The other three suffered from **tuberculosis** (too•ber•cu•LOW•sis) and struggled with illness their entire lives. Zeb, as he was nicknamed, was the only child in the Pike family to grow into a strong and healthy adult.

Zeb grew up in military posts on the American **frontier**. His father fought in the Revolutionary War and moved the family from place to place. Zeb never went to school, but he enjoyed reading and learned to speak French and Spanish. At the age of 15, Zeb joined his father's military **regiment** and helped drive Native Americans out of present-day Ohio.

ZEBULON PIKE'S NORTHWEST EXPEDITION

In the summer of 1805, while Lewis and Clark were exploring the West and searching for the Pacific Ocean, 26 year old Zebulon Pike was sent on an expedition of his own. He was instructed to travel northwest from St. Louis and find the source of the Mississippi River. He was also told to purchase Native American land for future military posts and bring Native American chiefs back to Missouri.

Zebulon Pike and 20 men left St. Louis and traveled up the Mississippi River in keelboats. During their nine month journey, the explorers traveled nearly 5,000 miles. Winter was especially difficult. They pushed and pulled their boats in freezing waters and nearly starved to death. Pike's expedition traveled as far north as Leech Lake in present-day Minnesota.

Zeb purchased more than 100,000 acres of land from the Sioux (SOO) tribe, but was unable to **convince** any of the Native American chiefs to return home with him. He never found the source of the Mississippi River.

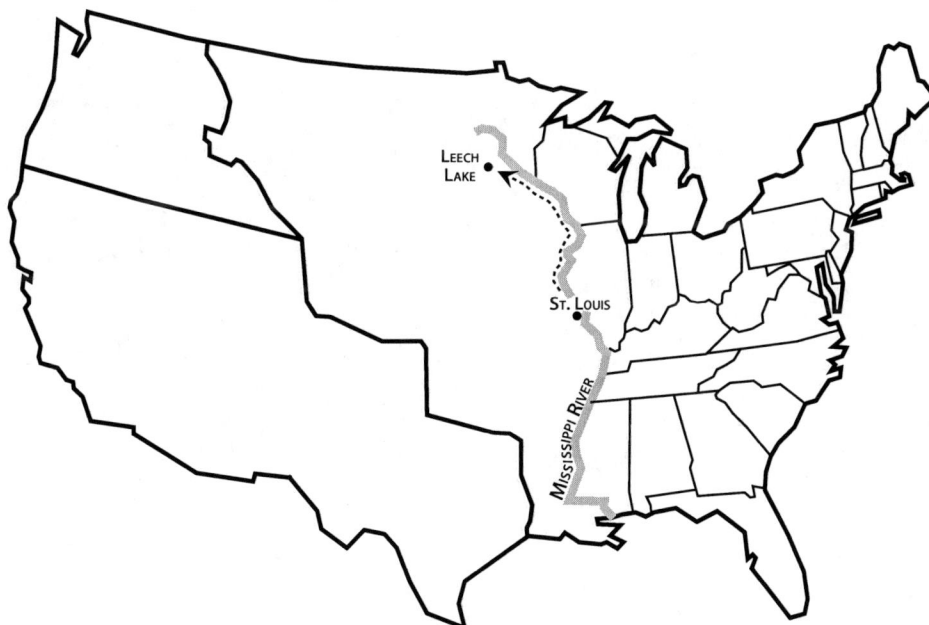

Zebulon Pike's Southwest Expedition

On April 30, 1806, Zeb and his men returned to St. Louis. Less than two months later, Zebulon Pike found himself leading an expedition to the Southwest. This time he was to explore the **headwaters** of the Arkansas River and follow it to the Red River before traveling down the Mississippi River. He was also instructed to spy on the Spanish who had settled on the southwestern border of the Louisiana Purchase.

On July 15, 1806, Zeb and 23 men left St. Louis and traveled up the Missouri River in keelboats. Their first mission was to return 51 Osage (OH•sayj) people to their villages in present-day Kansas. The Osage had been held **captive** by an eastern tribe. President Jefferson demanded that the Osage be returned home.

In Kansas, Zeb and his men traded their keelboats to the Native Americans who gave them horses. Guided by Osage warriors, the men traveled across Kansas until they reached the Arkansas River.

Zeb and his men made canoes out of buffalo skins. Winter was quickly approaching and Pike's men did not have the clothing, equipment, or supplies for a winter expedition. Instead of waiting until winter passed, Zeb made the bold decision to continue on. They set out in their canoes and followed the Arkansas River into Colorado. In Colorado, Zeb and a few soldiers split from the group and tried unsuccessfully to climb the tallest peak of a mountain they named Grand Peak.

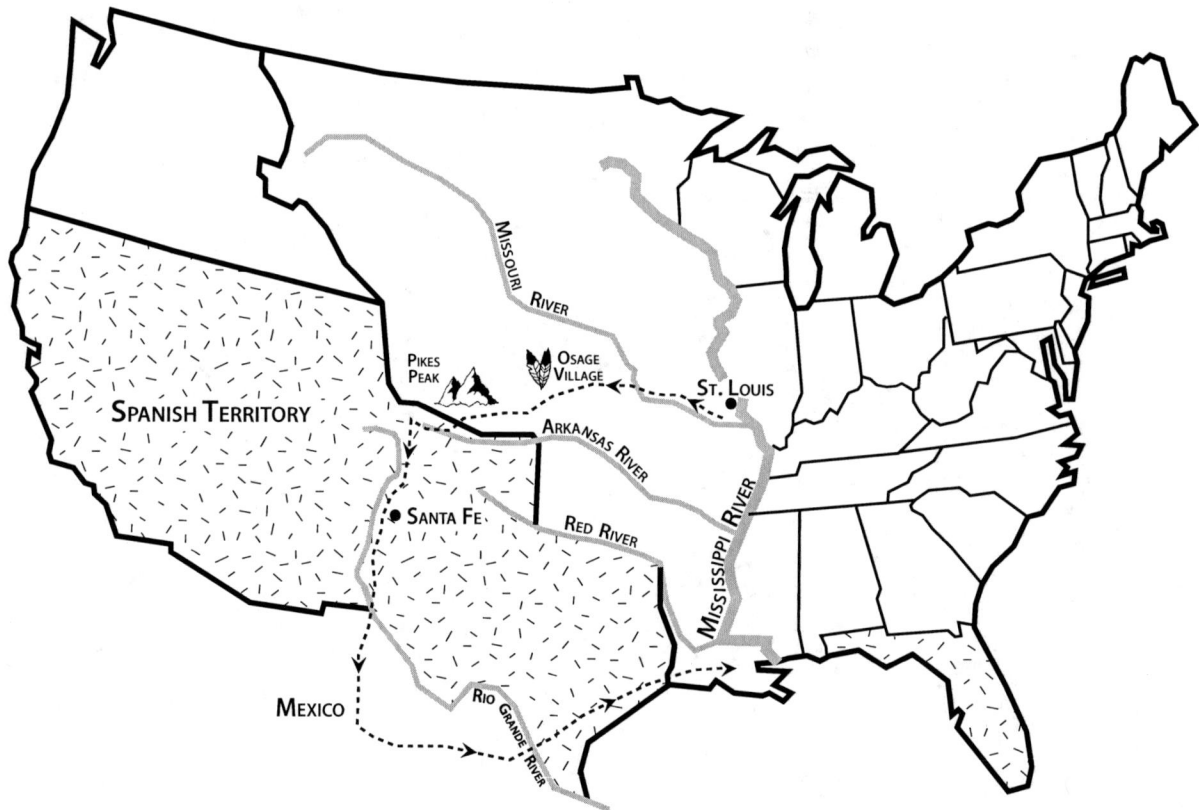

Pikes Peak

Zebulon Pike and his men were not prepared for the cold weather in Colorado or on Grand Peak. They suffered from hunger and nearly froze to death. Though they never reached the top of the 14,000 foot mountain, Grand Peak was later named Pikes Peak.

In 1807, the men continued their journey down the Arkansas River. Their food supplies ran out and they cut up the few blankets they had to use as socks. Since there were no maps of the region, Zeb and his men got lost. They ended up following the Rio Grande River into Spanish territory.

Spanish Capture

Spanish troops arrested Zebulon Pike and his men. They were marched first to Santa Fe, New Mexico, where they were questioned.

Zeb used the journey to Santa Fe to observe the placement of Spanish military forts, missions, and settlements. He made mental notes of the Spanish soldiers and officers.

After leaving Santa Fe, Pike and his men were led further south into Mexico. Zeb spent most of the journey talking with Spanish **priests** and gathering more information about the Spanish **culture**. He had successfully completed his mission to spy on the Spanish. Some **historians** wonder if Zeb planned on being captured so that he could spy on the Spanish.

In Mexico, Zeb was questioned by the Spanish **governor**. Afraid of angering the United States, the governor released Pike and his men. They were **escorted** to the United States border. Again, Zebulon Pike used the journey to take detailed notes about his surroundings.

Zebulon Montgomery Pike

Almost a year after his expedition started, Zebulon Pike arrived in New Orleans where he was met by his wife and young daughter. He brought with him the first detailed reports about the Spanish territory and two grizzly bear cubs that he gave to President Jefferson as gifts.

FAMOUS PEOPLE: ZEBULON MONTGOMERY PIKE

Name _____

Directions: Use the selection about Zebulon Pike to answer these questions. Circle the answers to questions 1 and 2. Write your answers on the lines provided for questions 3-5.

1   What can you learn by studying the map of Zebulon Pike's Southwest Expedition?

    A Santa Fe was north of Pikes Peak.

    B Zebulon Pike crossed the Arkansas River before crossing the Missouri River.

    C Pikes Peak was north of Santa Fe.

    D Zebulon Pike crossed the Red River twice.

2   Zebulon Pike was born in 1779 and climbed Pikes Peak in 1806. How old was Zeb when he climbed Pikes Peak?

    A 45

    B 27

    C 73

    D 37

3   During Zebulon Pike's first expedition to the Northwest, he purchased more than 100,000 acres from the Sioux tribe. Still, many people thought his expedition was a failure. Do you agree? Explain your reason.

_____

_____

_____

4   During Zebulon Pike's Southwest Expedition, he was captured by Spanish troops. Some historians believe he did this on purpose so that he could spy on the Spanish. What do you think? Would you have been captured on purpose? Explain.

_____

_____

_____

_____

5   Pikes Peak is named after Zebulon Pike. What famous place will be named after you someday? What will you do to deserve such an honor?

_____

_____

_____

Westward Expansion © 2009
splashpublications.com

28

Name _____

LEWIS And CLARK K·W·L·H CHART

PART II
DIRECTIONS:

1. Take out your unfinished Lewis and Clark Expedition K•W•L•H charts.

2. Use what you have read about the Lewis and Clark Expedition, books, encyclopedias, the Internet, and other **primary** and **secondary** sources to research and answer the five questions you asked about the Lewis and Clark Expedition. Write your answers in the "What I Learned" column of the charts.

3. List the book titles, encyclopedias, and website addresses that you used to find your information in the "How I Found Out" column of the charts.

4. Put a "P" next to the **primary sources** and an "S" next to the **secondary sources** that you used to find your information.

PART III

Use your K•W•L•H Charts to answer the questions below.

1   Based on your research, what is the most important <u>new</u> detail that you learned about the Lewis and Clark Expedition?

_____

_____

_____

2   Did your research change the way you thought about the Lewis and Clark Expedition? Explain your answer.

_____

_____

_____

_____

LEWIS And CLARK K·W·L·H CHART

PART IV

DIRECTIONS:

Use your finished Lewis and Clark K•W•L•H Chart to write a four or five sentence rough draft paragraph about Lewis and Clark on the back of this paper. Your paragraph should include the information from the "What I Learned" section of your K•W•L•H Chart.

Start your paragraph with a Topic Sentence and don't forget to end it with a good Closing Sentence.

Have your paragraph edited before neatly writing your final draft in the space below. Attach separate paper if you need more room.

❦❦❦❦❦❦ VOCABULARY QUIZ ❦❦❦❦❦❦
WESTWARD EXPANSION
PART III

DIRECTIONS: Match the vocabulary word on the left with its definition on the right. Put the letter for the definition on the blank next to the vocabulary word it matches. Use each word and definition only once.

1. _____ interpreter

2. _____ appendix

3. _____ tuberculosis

4. _____ astronomer

5. _____ tomahawks

6. _____ border

7. _____ surveyor

8. _____ historians

9. _____ botanist

10. _____ siblings

11. _____ captive

12. _____ regiment

13. _____ convince

14. _____ priests

15. _____ culture

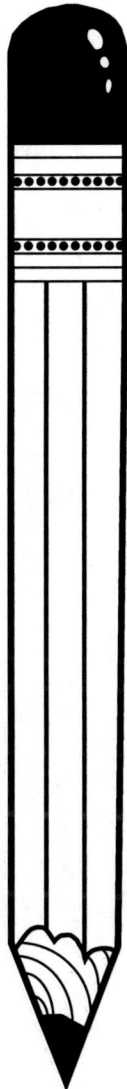

A.   a scientist who studies plants.

B.   people who study the past.

C.   a group of people with a shared set of beliefs, goals, religious customs, attitudes, and social practices.

D.   quickly moving bodies of water.

E.   a shallow covered river boat that is usually rowed or towed and used for carrying supplies.

F.   a prisoner who has been taken by force without permission.

G.   a military unit of ground troops.

H.   talk someone into doing something your way.

I.   a disease that attacks the lungs and causes fever.

J.   very unfriendly.

K.   someone who turns one language into another language so people speaking different languages can understand each other.

L.   brothers and sisters.

M.   lie right next to something.

16. _____ currents

17. _____ prairie

18. _____ escorted

19. _____ headwaters

20. _____ frontier

21. _____ hostile

22. _____ governor

23. _____ keelboat

N. a scientist who studies the stars and planets.

O. a person who is in charge of an area or group.

P. people with the authority to perform religious ceremonies.

Q. axes that were used as tools or weapons by some Native American tribes.

R. led away.

S. waters from which a river rises.

T. an area of land that has not yet been settled.

U. wide area of flat or rolling grassland.

V. a person who does a detailed inspection.

W. a small pouch located at the upper end of the large intestine.

THE SANTA FE TRAIL

The fur trade was one of the most important reasons for Europeans to travel to **North America**. During the 1600s and 1700s, the huge territory that would one day become the United States and Canada was explored. Land was claimed, wars were fought, and Native American cultures were destroyed in the **pursuit** of fur bearing animals.

Although beavers were the most popular fur bearing animals, muskrats, raccoons, foxes, deer, and buffalo were also hunted in the **Great Plains** and Great Lakes regions. In the **Pacific Northwest**, Russian and British traders hunted sea otters, whales, black bears, and even rats.

SEA OTTER

The skins of these animals were treated like cash. A deer hide, for example, was worth fifty cents or more. Eight buffalo robes could be traded for one riding horse. Thirty beaver **pelts** bought a keg of rum. For more than two **centuries**, the skins and hides of these animals were hunted and traded by the millions.

NATIVE AMERICANS AND THE FUR TRADE

Native Americans were very important to the success of the fur trade. They were skilled hunters who knew the best places to find fur bearing animals. In exchange for skins and pelts, the Native Americans were given European tools, alcohol, guns, and horses. **Competition** over trapping and trading areas was fierce. Fighting broke out between Native American tribes over control of the hunting territories and the valuable trade with the Europeans. The biggest and most organized tribes usually won.

Unfortunately, not everything brought to North America by the European traders was valuable to the Native Americans. **Infectious** diseases that included measles, chicken pox, **typhoid fever**, and **small pox** killed more than one million Native Americans. Alcohol was also responsible for many Native American illnesses and deaths. The Native Americans became **addicted** to the powerful drink.

Many tribes were willing to do almost anything to hunt for the white traders. They gave up their own hunting and stopped celebrating important religious **ceremonies**. Tribes that traded with the white trappers held the most power within the Native American villages.

MOUNTAIN MEN

In the late 1700s, long before the Louisiana Purchase, brave explorers from the United States and Canada began traveling west of the Mississippi River into Spanish-controlled territory. Their journey began in Missouri and took them to the Spanish capital of Santa Fe. They followed a winding path of Native American trails and rivers as they searched for fur bearing animals to trap and trade. These trappers and traders became known as mountain men.

THE LIFE OF A MOUNTAIN MAN

As you can imagine, the life of a mountain man was difficult and dangerous. The Spanish government didn't allow trade between its country and the United States. Getting caught could mean prison or even death. To survive in the wilderness, mountain men had to look like Native Americans. They dressed, walked, and even wore their hair like Native Americans. They traveled through all kinds of weather and fought off attacks from unfriendly Native Americans.

Everything that a mountain man owned had to be carried with him. He traveled by horse and could only pack the supplies he could carry. One hand guided the horse while the other hand held a rifle. Gunpowder, a bullet pouch, an axe, a sharp knife, beaver traps, blankets, food, and cooking supplies were rolled up in a small bundle and strapped to the horse.

THE SANTA FE TRAIL

In 1821, the Mexican settlers in Spain declared their independence. Like the 13 original English colonies, the Mexicans in Spain had grown tired of being told what to do by a country that was thousands of miles away. Spain and its colonists in Mexico went to war.

Spain lost the war and the Mexican government took control of the land west of the United States.

The Mexican government encouraged Americans to travel to Mexico. It even allowed them to trap and trade in Mexico.

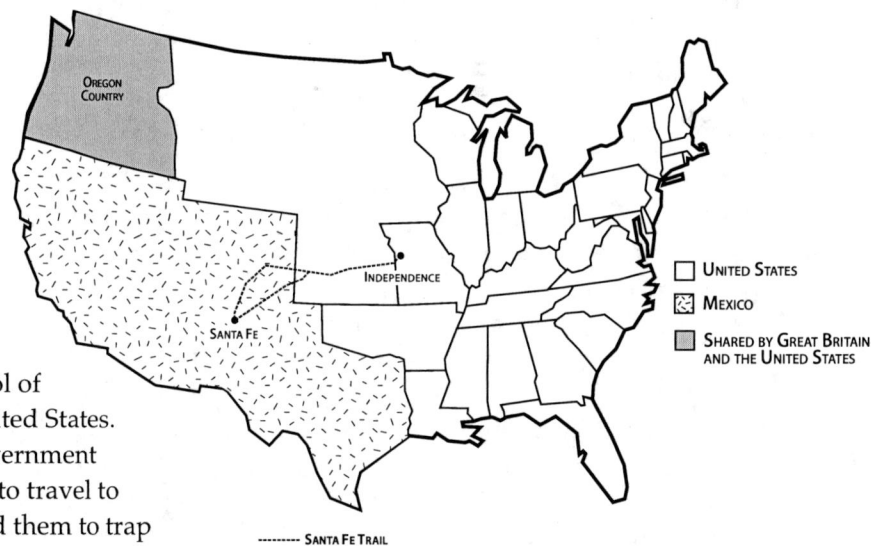

--------- SANTA FE TRAIL

The route traveled by the mountain men became known as the Santa Fe Trail. The 800-mile long trail snaked through Kansas and Colorado before ending in Santa Fe. During the next 20 years, the Santa Fe Trail led thousands of fur traders and a few brave American families in covered wagons to Mexico.

✦✦✦✦✦ THE SANTA FE TRAIL ✦✦✦✦✦

Directions: Read each question carefully. Darken the circle for the correct answer.

---

1 All of the following were popular animals hunted by the fur traders <u>except</u> –

   A beavers

   B rats

   C mules

   D black bears

2 After reading about the Native Americans and the fur trade, you get the idea that –

   F Native American tribes were willing to share hunting territories with other tribes

   G some of the things brought by European traders were harmful to Native Americans

   H tribes that traded with the white trappers were teased by other tribes

   J Native Americans were too busy with their own hunting and religious ceremonies to trade with the Europeans

3 Why did mountain men travel west of the Mississippi River into Santa Fe?

   A They wanted to claim land for their countries.

   B They wanted to live in Spain.

   C They were searching for fur bearing animals to trap and trade.

   D They wanted to help the Native Americans escape from Santa Fe.

4 In order to survive in the wilderness, mountain men had to –

   F look and act like Native Americans

   G pull wagons behind their horses

   H travel only during the summer

   J eat pancakes for breakfast

5 When Spain and its colonists in Mexico went to war, who won?

   A Spain

   B Great Britain

   C Mexico

   D The United States

6 After studying the Santa Fe Trail map, you learn that –

   F the mountain men traveled west from Independence

   G Santa Fe was east of Independence

   H the mountain men used the Santa Fe Trail to travel to Oregon Country

   J Santa Fe was part of the United States

7 According to the map of the Santa Fe Trail, Oregon Country was controlled by –

   A Mexico and the United States

   B Spain and France

   C Great Britain and the United States

   D France and Great Britain

READING

Answers

1 Ⓐ Ⓑ Ⓒ Ⓓ   5 Ⓐ Ⓑ Ⓒ Ⓓ

2 Ⓕ Ⓖ Ⓗ Ⓙ   6 Ⓕ Ⓖ Ⓗ Ⓙ

3 Ⓐ Ⓑ Ⓒ Ⓓ   7 Ⓐ Ⓑ Ⓒ Ⓓ

4 Ⓕ Ⓖ Ⓗ Ⓙ

FAMOUS PEOPLE: DANIEL BOONE

Daniel Boone was born on October 22, 1734. He was the sixth of eleven children in a family of **Quakers**. His father, Squire Boone, had **immigrated** to Pennsylvania from England in 1717.

Squire and his wife Sarah built a log cabin in Pennsylvania where Daniel and his siblings were born.

DANIEL BOONE'S EARLY LIFE

Daniel learned how to use a rifle at a very young age. He hunted with boys from nearby Native American villages.

Hunting took up most of Daniel's time and left little opportunity for him to go to school. He was taught to read and write from his older family members.

He often took the Bible and his favorite books with him on hunting trips. At night, Daniel would read aloud to his hunting **companions** around the light of the campfire.

At the age of 21, Daniel Boone fought in the French and Indian War. He and other colonists tried to drive the French and their Native American allies out of Ohio. After returning home, Daniel married Rebecca Bryan. The couple had 10 children.

THE LONG HUNTS

Hunting kept Daniel Boone away from his family for long periods of time. Almost every autumn, Boone would go on "long hunts," which took him deep into the wilderness for months. He hunted deer in the autumn and trapped beaver and otter during the winter. After returning from these hunting trips, Boone would sell the skins and pelts to fur traders.

DANIEL BOONE

It was during one of Daniel Boone's "long hunts" that he learned about present-day Kentucky. **Fertile** land and forests full of fur bearing animals attracted Boone to the area. Unfortunately, Kentucky was beyond the border of the 13 original colonies and off limits to British colonists. Great Britain had set this land aside for Native Americans after the French and Indian War.

ENTERING KENTUCKY

In May 1769, Daniel Boone **illegally** entered Kentucky through an area known as the Cumberland Gap. Boone and another hunter were captured by Shawnee warriors. The Shawnee took all of Boone's animal skins and furs. Daniel Boone was ordered to leave the area. Instead of leaving, Boone hid for awhile and then continued hunting and exploring Kentucky for the next two years.

On September 25, 1773, Boone led his family and 50 other **pioneers** through the Cumberland Gap into Kentucky.

The group turned back after being attacked by Native Americans. During the attack, Daniel Boone's oldest son James was **tortured** and killed by Native Americans.

The killing of Boone's son was one of the first events in what became known as Dunmore's War. Boone volunteered to help the colonists in Virginia battle the Shawnees for control of present-day West Virginia and Kentucky.

In the summer of 1774, Boone traveled 800 miles through the Kentucky wilderness to warn fur traders and trappers about the outbreak of war. In October, the Battle of Point Pleasant forced the Shawnees to give up their claims to Kentucky.

SHAWNEE WARRIOR

THE WILDERNESS ROAD

In 1775, Daniel Boone was hired to return to Kentucky and prepare the area for white settlement. Boone and a group of 30 men carved the famous Wilderness Road to the Kentucky River.

The Wilderness Road connected Native American trails and buffalo paths from eastern Virginia, through the Cumberland Gap, and into the present-day city of Lexington. Boone chose a spot at the end of the Wilderness Road and built a fort. He returned to North Carolina and brought his family to live in an area known today as Boonesboro.

Daniel Boone became one of the most famous pioneers in history. He spent his entire life exploring and settling the frontiers of America. His Wilderness Road later provided a route West for thousands of settlers. By 1800, more than 200,000 pioneers had traveled the Wilderness Road as they made their journeys West.

FAMOUS PEOPLE: DANIEL BOONE

Directions: Use the selection about Daniel Boone to answer these questions. Circle the answers to questions 1 and 2. Write your answers on the lines provided for questions 3-5.

1   After reading about Daniel Boone's early life, you learn that –

   A   he was the father of 10 children

   B   he was afraid of guns

   C   he graduated from high school at a very young age

   D   he was never married

2   Daniel Boone was born in 1734 and carved the famous Wilderness Road in 1775. How old was Daniel Boone when he carved the Wilderness Road?

   A   41

   B   59

   C   21

   D   46

3   Daniel Boone was one of eleven children. What do you think are the advantages of being born into such a large family? What are the disadvantages?

   advantages _____

   _____

   disadvantages _____

   _____

4   In 1769, Daniel Boone illegally traveled to Kentucky. Even after being caught and told to leave the area, he stayed. Why do you think Daniel Boone continued to do something that he knew was wrong?

   _____

   _____

   _____

5   Daniel Boone paid a very high price for entering Kentucky illegally. His son was killed by Native Americans. Describe a time that you did something wrong and got caught. Did your punishment keep you from doing wrong again? Explain.

   _____

   _____

   _____

   _____

THE PACIFIC NORTHWEST

The Pacific Northwest includes the present-day states of Washington, Idaho, Oregon, Montana, and the Canadian **province** of British Columbia. The land in the Pacific Northwest was first **inhabited** by Native Americans.

Tribes that lived west of the Cascade Mountains built large villages with permanent homes made of cedar boards. They fished for salmon in the rivers and streams, hunted whales in the Pacific Ocean, and took time for **recreation** and celebrations.

An endless supply of food, plenty of natural **resources**, and a mild **climate** gave Native Americans living west of the Cascade Mountains a very comfortable life.

Life was very different east of the Cascade Mountains. The summers were hotter and the winters were colder. There were very few trees and food was difficult to find. Temporary homes were built partly below ground for protection from the heat and cold. Most of the Native Americans' time was spent searching for food.

BLUE WHALE

During the summer, trips were made to gather roots, berries, seeds, and other wild plants. In the fall, men left their homes to hunt for deer, rabbits, mountain goats, elk, and birds. Life was very difficult for Native Americans east of the Cascade Mountains.

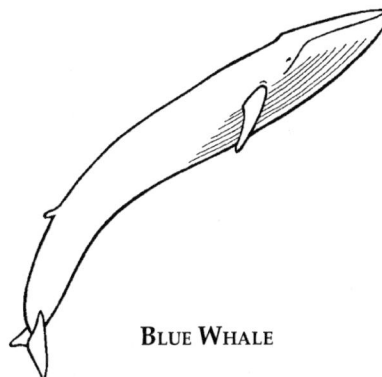

THE NORTHWEST PASSAGE

The first European explorers to visit the Pacific Northwest were not interested in fur bearing animals or claiming land for their countries. They were trying to find the Northwest Passage. The Northwest Passage was a water route that explorers hoped connected North America to **Asia**.

Getting to Asia was very important to European explorers. In Asia, they could buy jewels, silk, and spices that were not available in Europe. The only way to get these items was to buy them from Italian traders. The Italian traders purchased the items in Asia and sold them at very high prices to Europeans. If explorers found a water route to Asia, they could buy the things they wanted without paying Italian traders anything.

ROUTES TO ASIA

Most European explorers followed an eastward route to Asia. They started in Europe and sailed around the tip of Africa. Violent storms in this part of the Atlantic Ocean made this route very dangerous.

Many explorers from Spain, France, and England tried and failed to find the Northwest Passage. This is because the Northwest Passage did not exist. As you can see by looking at the map below, there is no direct water route connecting North America and Asia; land is in the way.

In 1492, Christopher Columbus sailed west from Europe to an area that he thought was Asia. He claimed the land for Spain and was so certain he had reached the East Indies, he named the strange people he met Indians. Today, we know that Christopher Columbus did not reach Asia. He found an area that we call the West Indies.

During the 1600s, French explorers Samuel de Champlain (sham•PLANE) and Robert La Salle tried finding the Northwest Passage. Both sailed west from France and built French colonies in present-day Canada before beginning their searches for the Northwest Passage. Champlain sailed as far as Lake Huron, the second largest of North America's five Great Lakes. Instead of finding the Northwest Passage, La Salle sailed down the Mississippi River and claimed all of the land around the river for France.

In 1609, English explorer Henry Hudson tried his luck at finding the Northwest Passage. Although he was only 700 miles from the North Pole and farther north than any other explorer before him, Hudson lost his life trying to find the Northwest Passage.

——— EASTERN ROUTE TO ASIA

- - - - CHRISTOPHER COLUMBUS'S ROUTE TO "ASIA"

------- SAMUEL CHAMPLAIN'S AND ROBERT LASALLE'S ROUTES TO "ASIA"

········· HENRY HUDSON'S ROUTE TO "ASIA"

CONTROL OF THE PACIFIC NORTHWEST

After the Louisiana Purchase, President Thomas Jefferson sent explorers Meriwether Lewis and William Clark to explore the Pacific Northwest. Lewis and Clark found that the Pacific Northwest was filled with fish and fur bearing animals that included beavers, raccoons, black bears, and sea otters.

Of course, explorers from Spain and Great Britain also found the area rich in natural resources and fur bearing animals.

By the early 1800s, Spain, Great Britain, and the United States claimed ownership of the Pacific Northwest.

In 1810, the North West Company, a British owned fur trading company, sent a group of men into the Pacific Northwest to buy furs from the Native Americans. They built Spokane House, a trading post near the present-day city of Spokane. A year later, Americans built Fort Okanogan (oh•kuh•NAH•gan).

Fur trading caused a lot of **tension** between Great Britain and the United States in the Pacific Northwest and the present-day states just south of Canada. Since the Revolutionary War, Americans believed that the British living in Canada were encouraging the Native Americans to attack white settlements to the south. It was true. In exchange for beaver furs, the British supplied the Native Americans with weapons and **ammunition**.

THE WAR OF 1812

In 1812, the United States declared war on Great Britain. The United States planned to take over Canada and permanently end Great Britain's **influence** over the Native Americans. The War of 1812 was strongly supported by American citizens. Supply routes were organized and forts were built to **defend** the areas of the United States that bordered British-controlled Canada.

The Americans successfully defeated Great Britain's soldiers during many battles of the war. After almost three years of fighting, a peace treaty was signed by the United States and Great Britain. Neither side won any land during the War of 1812. The war ended Great Britain's influence over the Native Americans. It also marked the last time that the United States and Great Britain would ever go to war against each other.

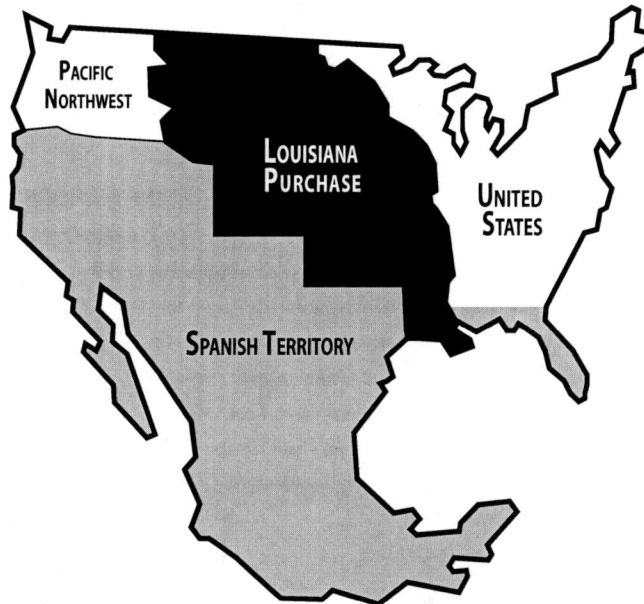

THE HUDSON'S BAY COMPANY

By 1818, Great Britain and the United States had signed another treaty. To avoid **conflict** and another possible war, Great Britain and the United States agreed that people from both countries could trade and settle in the region called Oregon Country. Not wanting to go to war with either country, Spain signed a treaty giving up its claim to the Pacific Northwest.

For many years, it seemed that Great Britain would control Oregon Country. In 1821, English fur traders from the Hudson's Bay Company were sent to the Pacific Northwest. They established their **headquarters** on the Columbia River in present-day Vancouver, Washington. They built several buildings surrounded by a high fence made of logs. They named their headquarters Fort Vancouver.

Fort Vancouver was almost like a small city. At one point, there were at least 27 buildings and hundreds of residents living at Fort Vancouver. The settlers trapped fur bearing animals. They traded with the nearby Native Americans. Families grew fruit trees and crops of wheat, oats, and barley. They also raised farm animals. They kept what they needed and sold the rest. It was a very successful business for them.

JOHN MCLOUGHLIN

John McLoughlin was in charge of the Hudson's Bay Company. He ran the fur trading business and took control of the activities at Fort Vancouver.

McLoughlin decided where the fur hunters would go and how much to trade for furs. He helped people in need and punished those who broke the rules.

McLoughlin was known as the "White-Headed Eagle" to the Native Americans in the area. He treated the Native Americans with **respect**. McLoughlin made sure that everyone at Fort Vancouver treated the Native Americans fairly.

JOHN MCLOUGHLIN

During the 1820s, John McLoughlin was seen as the most powerful person in the Pacific Northwest. He was told by Great Britain's leaders to keep Americans from settling in Oregon Country. Instead, McLoughlin gave Americans food, money, and advice. Many Americans owed their success and their lives to John McLoughlin's help and **generosity**. After **retiring** from fur trading, McLoughlin himself became an American citizen.

News of fur bearing animals made more American fur traders want to travel West. You will soon learn about the trail that brought American trappers and settlers into the Pacific Northwest. You will also discover how the United States finally took full control of the area that helped our nation expand to its present-day boundaries in the Northwest.

Name _____

THE PACIFIC NORTHWEST

Directions: Read each question carefully. Darken the circle for the correct answer.

1 **Which of the following is not a present-day state in the Pacific Northwest?**

 A Washington

 B Idaho

 C Montana

 D Ohio

2 **Which phrase tells you that Native Americans living east of the Cascade Mountains had a difficult life?**

 F ...large villages with homes made of cedar boards...

 G ...took time for recreation and celebrations...

 H ...very few trees and food was difficult to find...

 J ...hunted whales in the Pacific Ocean...

3 **Why was discovering the Northwest Passage so important to European explorers?**

 A They wanted to pay Italian traders more money.

 B They wanted to live in Asia.

 C The Northwest Passage would help them find South America.

 D They wanted to travel to Asia so they could buy items that were not available in Europe.

4 **How did most European explorers travel to Asia?**

 F They sailed west from Europe.

 G They sailed to the West Indies.

 H They sailed around the tip of Africa.

 J They sailed through the Great Lakes.

5 **What was wrong with this route to Asia?**

 A It took too long.

 B Land was in the way.

 C They had to fight off hostile Native Americans.

 D Violent storms made this route very dangerous.

6 **Which statement about the War of 1812 is true?**

 F Great Britain won the War of 1812.

 G The War of 1812 was the last time that Great Britain and the United States ever went to war against each other.

 H The War of 1812 started when Great Britain declared war on the United States.

 J The United States won the War of 1812.

7 **What can you learn from reading about John McLoughlin?**

 A He was a very selfish man who rarely helped anyone.

 B He treated Native Americans very poorly.

 C He didn't always listen to what government leaders told him to do.

 D After retiring from fur trading, he became a French citizen.

READING

Answers

1 Ⓐ Ⓑ Ⓒ Ⓓ   5 Ⓐ Ⓑ Ⓒ Ⓓ
2 Ⓕ Ⓖ Ⓗ Ⓙ   6 Ⓕ Ⓖ Ⓗ Ⓙ
3 Ⓐ Ⓑ Ⓒ Ⓓ   7 Ⓐ Ⓑ Ⓒ Ⓓ
4 Ⓕ Ⓖ Ⓗ Ⓙ

FAMOUS PEOPLE: THE MAKAH

The Makah people lived in five villages on the Olympic **Peninsula** in the far northwest corner of present-day Washington. They were one of the few tribes west of the Cascade Mountains to take on the dangerous job of whale hunting.

PREPARING FOR THE WHALE HUNT

To the Makah, whale hunting was a **ritual**. To prepare for the **annual** spring whale hunt, skilled carvers made canoes for the hunters. Each canoe was carved from a cedar tree. It was fifty feet long and eight feet wide. A single canoe could hold 20 hunters and everything needed to bring home a whale. As the day of the whale hunt drew near, the whalers and their wives **fasted**, bathed, and prayed.

THE WHALE HUNT

When the day arrived, the hunters gathered on the beach. Once a whale was spotted, the whalers jumped into their cedar canoes. The hunters paddled right up next to the huge animal. There was no room for mistakes. When the time was right, the chief hunter plunged his wooden **harpoon** into the whale's side. The harpoon had a **barbed** tip that stuck into the whale's flesh. A long line with sealskin floats was tied to the other end of the harpoon. The floats slowed the whale so it could not swim away as quickly. Still, the whale dove and tried with all of its might to get away.

GRAY WHALE

The hunters paddled quickly and sang songs, trying to get the huge animal to swim toward the shore. When the whale dove downward, the men tied on more lines with floats. As the whale grew tired, more men arrived in canoes to help kill the huge animal.

Everyone in the village came to meet the canoes. They gave thanks for a safe hunt. Every part of the whale was used. Nothing was ever wasted. The meat was eaten. The oil was used for cooking and making foods taste better. The teeth were used for making jewelry. The skeleton of the whale was used for building.

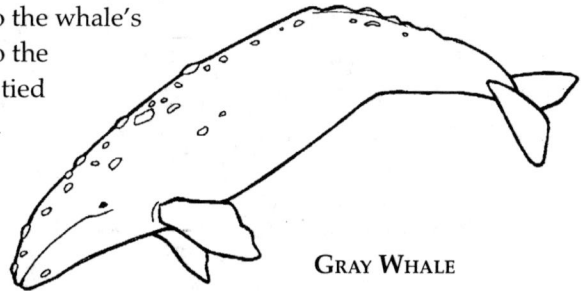

THE OZETTE MUD SLIDE

About 500 years ago, a mud slide completely buried the Makah whaling village near the present-day town of Ozette. In 1970, scientists discovered the hidden village. More than 55,000 **artifacts** including buildings, skeletons, tools, **sculptures**, and baskets had been perfectly **preserved** underneath the thick layers of mud.

Descendants of the Makah people continue to live on the Olympic Peninsula. Although it is illegal to hunt whales today, the Makah Nation was permitted to go on a gray whale hunt in 1999.

FAMOUS PEOPLE: THE MAKAH

Directions: Use the selection about the Makah people to answer these questions. Circle the answers to questions 1 and 2. Write your answers on the lines provided for questions 3-5.

---

1   How were the Makah people different from most of the other Coastal tribes?

   A   They hunted whales.

   B   They carved canoes from cedar trees.

   C   They gave thanks for the food that they hunted.

   D   They lived in villages.

2   After reading about the Makah people, you get the idea that –

   A   they were afraid of whales

   B   they hunted whales three or four times each year

   C   they were willing to risk their lives to hunt for whales

   D   after eating the meat, they threw the rest of the whale away

3   The Coastal people had plenty of food, yet the Makah took on the dangerous job of hunting whales. Why do you think they risked their lives to hunt whales?

_____

_____

4   Describe how the Makah people killed a whale.

_____

_____

_____

5   About 500 years ago, a mud slide completely buried the Makah village. Scientists learned about the Makah people from more than 50,000 artifacts found under the layers of mud. If a mud slide covered your community, what <u>two</u> artifacts would scientists find to teach others about your life 500 years from now? Explain the importance of these artifacts.

_____

_____

_____

_____

_____

FAMOUS PEOPLE: ROBERT GRAY

Robert Gray was born in Rhode Island on May 10, 1755. Little is known of Robert's early life, but it was reported that as a young man he served in the **Continental Army** during the Revolutionary War.

GRAY'S FIRST VOYAGE TO THE PACIFIC NORTHWEST

In 1787, Captain Robert Gray made his first **voyage** to the Pacific Northwest. He and Captain John Kendrick left Boston in two ships loaded with blankets, knives, American coins, and other gifts to trade with the Native Americans. Kendrick and Gray sailed south around the southern tip of South America before heading north toward the Pacific Northwest.

Violent storms damaged Captain Kendrick's ship, forcing Captain Gray to sail into the Pacific Northwest alone. Captain Kendrick soon joined him and the two explored the coastlines of present-day California, Oregon, Washington, and British Columbia. They traded their American gifts to the Native Americans for sea otter pelts and other animal furs.

THE COLUMBIA RIVER

In 1788, Robert Gray tried to navigate his ship through a large river. The current was too strong and the **tides** too high for Gray's ship to make it into the river's opening. The body of water was the present-day Columbia River.

The Columbia River enters the United States from Canada and flows south through the present-day state of Washington. It forms the boundaries of Oregon and Washington before emptying into the Pacific Ocean.

For centuries, explorers searching for the Northwest Passage missed the opening to the Columbia River. Of course, the river was no secret to the Native Americans. They had been living beside and using the Columbia River's resources for hundreds of years. The Native Americans called the river Ouragon.

Like others before him, Captain Robert Gray was not able to enter the Columbia River. It was just too dangerous. He sailed his ship on to China where he traded the otter pelts and animal furs for tea, spices, and other Chinese items. On August 9, 1790, Robert Gray returned safely to Boston, becoming the first American to **circumvent** the globe.

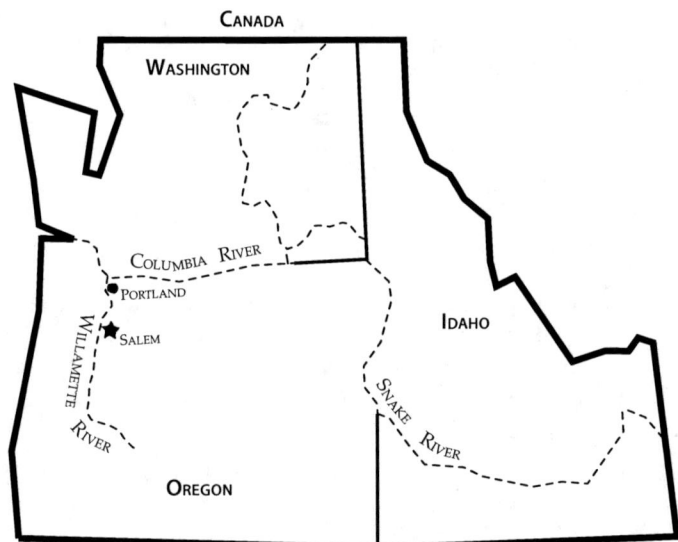

Gray's Second Voyage to the Pacific Northwest

Six weeks after arriving back in Boston, Captain Robert Gray set sail for his second voyage to the Pacific Northwest. He arrived a year later and spent nine days trying to enter the Columbia River.

Once again, the currents at the opening of the river were too strong for Gray's ship.

Captain Gray spent the winter on Vancouver Island in present-day British Columbia and waited for the cold weather to pass.

Native Americans did not welcome Captain Gray and his crew. Some of his men, including his son, were murdered by hostile Native Americans. Gray and his men were forced to keep constant guard to avoid further attacks.

In April 1792, Robert Gray tried once again to navigate his ship through the opening of the Columbia River. The shifting **sand bars** at the mouth of the river made entry impossible.

Entering the Columbia River

Captain Gray sailed north and spent time in present-day Grays **Harbor** before returning to the river. This time, he successfully sailed a small sailboat across the sand bars and into the river's **estuary**. Gray named the large river Columbia after his ship.

CAPTAIN ROBERT GRAY

Robert Gray navigated the sailboat up the Columbia River where he met Native Americans in canoes. Gray and his crew exchanged nails and other small items for otter pelts, salmon, and deer meat. Gray's crew gathered more than 450 animal furs before sailing on to China to trade for more tea and spices.

At the time, Robert Gray and many others did not think his discovery of the Columbia River was very important. He was not sent on any other voyages. He did not receive any **recognition** or wealth for his discovery. In 1806, Robert Gray died in **poverty**.

We know today that Robert Gray's discovery of the Columbia River was very important. It opened a new trade route for the United States. Most importantly, Captain Gray's discovery would one day help the United States claim Oregon Country for itself.

FAMOUS PEOPLE: ROBERT GRAY

Directions: Use the selection about Robert Gray to answer these questions. Circle the answers to questions 1 and 2. Write your answers on the lines provided for questions 3-6.

1 Robert Gray was born in 1755 and discovered the Columbia River in 1792. How old was Robert Gray when he discovered the Columbia River?

   A 47

   B 37

   C 43

   D 26

2 After studying the map of the Columbia River, you learn that –

   A the Columbia River runs south of Portland

   B the Willamette River runs east of the Columbia River

   C the Snake River runs west of the Columbia River

   D the Columbia River runs west of the Snake River

3 Robert Gray attempted to enter the Columbia River several times without success, yet he kept trying until he was successful. What are you hoping to be successful at this year?

_____

_____

4 Robert Gray's son was killed during his second attempt to successfully enter the Columbia River. What are you willing to give up to be successful?

_____

_____

5 Do you think there are times when a person should give up trying to be successful at something? Explain why you feel this way.

_____

_____

_____

6 If you aren't successful, will you quit or keep trying the way Robert Gray did? Explain your reason for quitting or continuing.

_____

_____

_____

PACIFIC NORTHWEST EXPERT'S JOURNAL

Explorers who traveled to the Pacific Northwest saw many different **species** of **mammals** and birds. They took careful notes and kept detailed journals about the animals they saw.

In this activity, you will get the chance to explore the Pacific Northwest and become an expert about mammals and birds that you will see during your expedition. You will use your information to create an *Expert's Journal* that includes pictures and descriptions of each type of animal.

To complete your *Pacific Northwest Expert's Journal*, you will need:

- information about animals of the Pacific Northwest.
- pages with the pictures of mammals and birds already on them.
- coloring pencils.
- scissors.
- two pieces of light colored construction paper to make a front and back cover for your book.
- use of a stapler.

DIRECTIONS:

1. Use the 14 mammal and bird pages and your information about the Pacific Northwest mammals and birds to correctly color each of the 14 animals.

2. Use your information about the Pacific Northwest's mammals and birds and the lines provided on each of the pages to fill in the required information about each animal. Spelling Counts!

3. When you are finished with all 14 mammals and birds, arrange the pages neatly on top of each other.

4. Use your coloring pencils to neatly decorate one piece of construction paper for the front cover of your *Pacific Northwest Expert's Journal*.

5. Place the front cover on the top and the back cover on the bottom.

6. Staple your *Pacific Northwest Expert's Journal* along the left side of the cover.

MAMMALS

BLACK BEAR

Black bears are **omnivores** that roam through the forests and **mountainous** areas of the Pacific Northwest. They can usually be seen near rivers and lakes where they find plenty of fish and insects. The fur color of black bears can actually be black, tan, brown, or yellow. Black bears can run up to 30 miles per hour and are excellent climbers. They have poor eyesight, but their hearing is good and their sense of smell is excellent. Full grown black bears are some of the largest mammals in North America. At birth, black bear cubs are blind and only weigh about eight ounces. Adult females can weigh as much as 600 pounds. Full grown males can weigh a whopping 1,200 pounds! During the cold winter months, black bears find a quiet place at the base of a tree or under the ledge of a large rock. They remain **inactive** for part of the winter. To prepare for this period of inactivity, black bears eat more than 20,000 calories a day. These extra calories add layers of fat so they can get through the long winter. Compare this with the fact that an average human being eats between 2,000 and 3,000 calories per day. Humans are the only enemies of black bears, so as you explore the Pacific Northwest, don't try to feed them or get near them.

The Pacific Northwest used to have a large number of bighorn sheep. During the 1930s, over hunting and disease nearly destroyed all of these mammals. Bighorn sheep have extremely good eyesight, very short tails, and pointed ears. Male bighorn sheep are known as rams. Female bighorn sheep are ewes. Their babies are called lambs. The horns of rams are larger and curlier than the horns of ewes. Rams often use their horns in battle with each other. They run up to 30 miles per hour before crashing head-on into another ram. Unlike most other types of sheep, bighorn sheep are covered with an outer layer of brown hair instead of wool. The underparts of bighorn sheep are gray and their tails are white.

BIGHORN SHEEP

Mountain Lion

Mountain lions are the largest wildcats in the United States. They are also known as cougars, pumas, or panthers. Mountain lions can be found in the forests and mountainous areas of the Pacific Northwest. There they can hide from **predators** that include bears, other mountain lions, and wolves. Mountain lions are most active at night when they hunt for mule deer, porcupines, and other small animals. Adult mountain lions will eat up to 30 pounds of meat at one meal. Mother mountain lions teach their kittens to hunt by practicing on **rodents** and rabbits. Mountain lions have thick brownish-orange coats and small rounded black-tipped ears. The tips of their tails are also black.

Elk, or wapiti, are the largest deer in the Pacific Northwest. Elk can be easily spotted in the high mountains and low valleys of the Pacific Northwest by their large bodies and huge horns. Their body colors can range from light tan to dark brown. They are **herbivores** that eat mostly grass and herbs. In the late 1800s, the elk population in the United States was almost completely wiped out. They were being killed for their hides, antlers, or sometimes just their **canine** teeth, which are made of ivory. Today, hunters must buy a permit and follow strict rules to hunt elk.

Elk

Mountain Goat

Mountain goats live high up in steep rocky cliffs and ledges. During the summer, mountain goats have short white woolly coats with bearded chins. In the winter, their fur thickens and turns yellow. Both males, known as billies, and females, known as nannies, have curved black horns that grow about ten inches long. Mountain goats are known for their speed. They are able to climb steep cliffs quickly and easily. Their hooves are soft and curved. They act like suction cups in rocky areas. Baby mountain goats, known as kids, are able to walk and jump around only 10 minutes after birth.

FAST FACTS

- Gray whales are popular mammals spotted in the Pacific Northwest. They are often found within a mile or two of the coastal shore. Because of this, they were easy targets for Native American hunters who killed gray whales for their oil, meat, hide, and **baleen**. Today, it is illegal to hunt and kill gray whales.
- In the wild, sea lions usually live about 15 years. You can tell how old a sea lion is by counting the number of rings on cross sections of its teeth.

CALIFORNIA SEA LION

California sea lions inhabit the Pacific waters from Canada to Mexico. They are members of the walking seal family. Sea lions are known for their intelligence, playfulness, and noisy barking. They use their large flippers to "walk" on land. Full grown male sea lions are chocolate brown in color and can weigh as much as 1,000 pounds. Adult females are light golden brown in color and weigh about 220 pounds. Sea lions spend time on land and in the water. They dive as deep as 400 feet in search of mollusks, squid, octopus, and small sharks. Killer whales and great white sharks **prey** upon California sea lions. Their main enemies are fishing nets that accidentally trap and kill sea lions before they can be released.

Ringtails are small mammals weighing only two pounds. They are also known as "miners' cats" because during the Gold Rush they were often found near mining camps. Today, ringtails are located near river valleys or springs where water can easily be found. Their most striking features are their tails, which are as long as their grayish-brown bodies and striped with black and white rings. They are very good climbers and their tails help them keep their balance. Their ankles can rotate, allowing them to go head first down a cliff or tree. Ringtails hunt for food at night. They eat mice, birds, and insects.

RINGTAIL

HARBOR SEAL

Harbor seals are found on the Pacific Coast. They are five to six feet long and can weigh up to 300 pounds. Harbor seals split their time evenly between land and water. They can dive up to 1,500 feet for up to 40 minutes. They are usually seen diving for about seven minutes in **shallow** waters. Harbor seals are true seals because they have small flippers. They must move on land by flopping along on their bellies. Harbor seals have spotted coats in a variety of shades from reddish to silver-gray or dark brown. They feed on fish, squid, and small sharks. Harbor seal pups are born in late spring. Pups weigh about 30 pounds. They can swim immediately after birth.

BIRDS

Great horned owls can be found throughout the Pacific Northwest. They have yellow eyes, dark bills, and white patches under their throats. Their bodies are streaked with colors of brown, black, and gray. Great horned owls are only 20 inches long, but they have wingspans of 55 inches. If you stretched out your arms and measured the length from the longest finger on your left hand to the longest finger on your right hand, you would get a pretty good idea of a great horned owl's wingspan. Great horned owls build their nests high in trees. They also have been known to steal the nests of hawks, eagles, or crows. Females lay two or three grayish-white eggs that hatch in about 30 days. Young great horned owls leave their nests 60 days later. Like most owls, great horned owls eat small mammals. They are also able to turn their heads completely around without moving their bodies.

GREAT HORNED OWL

Bald eagles can be found living near areas with plenty of water. Bald eagles eat fish, plucked from the water with their sharp **talons**. They also eat **waterfowl**, rodents, birds, and rabbits. Bald eagles have white heads and upper necks, white tails, dark brown bodies, and yellow bills. Their nests can be seven to eight feet across and are usually built in tall trees, high above the ground. Females lay one to three eggs. Both parents take turns keeping the eggs warm for about 35 days. Like great horned owls, bald eagles have wingspans almost three times the lengths of their bodies. Adult bald eagles are 32 inches long, but their wingspans measure 80 inches.

BALD EAGLE

Large numbers of peregrine falcons nest in the Pacific Northwest. Adult peregrine falcons have dark bluish-gray upperparts and wings. Their underparts are whitish-tan in color. Peregrine falcons usually choose to build their nests on cliffs and rock ledges that are close to water and prey. They hunt for smaller birds and even eat bats that they are able to catch in mid-air. In April, peregrine falcons lay eggs that hatch in about 35 days. Young peregrine falcons remain in the nest for another 45 days. They stay close to their parents for another four months after they are born.

PEREGRINE FALCON

Double-crested cormorants are commonly seen nesting in the harbors on the Pacific Coast. They choose these spots along the Pacific Coast where they can dive up to 25 feet below the water's surface in search of fish. Double-crested cormorants have long, thin necks. Their large, rounded throat pouches are orange in color. Adults are black with gray tipped wings. They have straight yellow bills that are hooked at the end. Both parents work together to build the nest. They take turns sitting on eggs that hatch 25 days after being laid. Baby double-crested cormorants wander from their nests about 25 days later to begin finding their own food.

DOUBLE-CRESTED CORMORANT

Mountain chickadees can be spotted in the Pacific Northwest just east of the Cascade Mountains. They are small birds about four inches long. They have light gray bodies and dark gray wings. The tops of their heads and throats are black. They also have black rings around their eyes and white eyebrows. Female mountain chickadees lay about eight spotted or white eggs in a fur-lined nest built inside of a woodpecker hole. The eggs hatch in about 14 days. The young chickadees leave the nest 21 days later. Mountain chickadees are constantly moving in search of insects living in the forest's trees.

MOUNTAIN CHICKADEE

Yellow warblers are tiny birds with greenish-yellow wings, tails, and legs. They have plain yellow faces with yellow rings around their dark eyes. Yellow warblers eat mostly insects and fruit. They can be seen singing in many areas of the Pacific Northwest. Yellow warblers choose trees to build nests of grass, bark, plants, and fur. Females lay one to seven greenish-white eggs that hatch about 12 days later. Within two weeks, the young yellow warblers are ready to leave the nest.

YELLOW WARBLER

BLACK BEAR

Black bears are large mammals in the Pacific Northwest. They are omnivores that usually roam the mountains and forests.

Omnivores are _____

_____

_____

_____

Black bears only weigh about eight ounces at birth. Full grown females can weigh

_____

and full grown males can weigh _____

_____

The fur colors of black bears can be _____

_____

_____

Two interesting facts about black bears are _____

_____

_____

_____

_____

_____

_____

_____

BIGHORN SHEEP

The Pacific Northwest used to have a large number of bighorn sheep, but during the 1930s, the population was nearly destroyed by _____

_____

_____

_____

_____

Male bighorn sheep are known as _____

Female bighorn sheep are known as _____

Unlike most other types of sheep, bighorn sheep are covered with _____

_____

The underparts of bighorn sheep are _____

and their tails are _____

Two interesting facts about bighorn sheep are _____

_____

_____

_____

_____

_____

_____

_____

MOUNTAIN LION

Mountain lions are the largest wildcats in the United States. They are also known as _____

_____

_____

In the Pacific Northwest, mountain lions can be found _____

_____

_____

They hunt for _____

_____

Predators of mountain lions include _____

_____

_____

Two interesting facts about mountain lions are _____

_____

_____

_____

_____

_____

_____

_____

_____

ELK

Elk are large deer-like herbivores.

Herbivores are _____

_____

_____

_____

_____

Elk can be easily spotted by _____

_____

_____

In the Pacific Northwest, elk can be found _____

_____

_____

They eat mostly _____

_____

Two interesting facts about elk are _____

_____

_____

_____

_____

_____

_____

_____

_____

MOUNTAIN GOAT

Mountain goats live high up in steep rocky cliffs and ledges. Male mountain goats are known as _____

_____

Female mountain goats are known as_____

_____

and baby mountain goats are known as _____

_____

Mountain goats are known for their speed and ability to _____

_____

Their hooves are _____

and act like _____

Two interesting facts about mountain goats are_____

_____

_____

_____

_____

_____

_____

_____

CALIFORNIA SEA LION

California sea lions inhabit the Pacific

waters from _____

_____

They are members of the walking seal

family and are known for _____

_____

_____

_____

Sea lions are preyed upon by_____

_____

but their main enemies are_____

_____

Two interesting facts about California sea lions are_____

_____

_____

_____

_____

_____

_____

_____

_____

RINGTAIL

Ringtails are small mammals weighing only two pounds. They are also known

as _____

because _____

_____

_____

Today, ringtails are located _____

_____

_____

Their most striking features are their _____

which are_____

_____

_____

Two interesting facts about ringtails are _____

_____

_____

_____

_____

_____

_____

_____

_____

_____

HARBOR SEAL

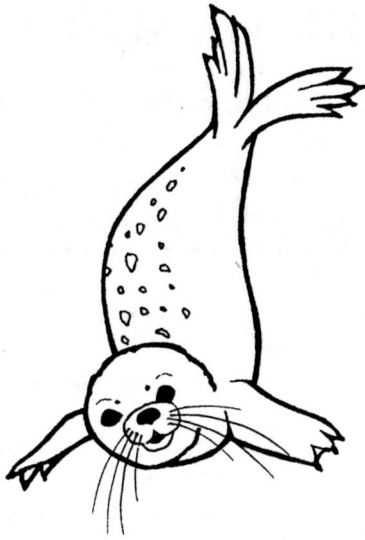

Harbor seals are found _____

_____

They split their time evenly between

_____

_____

Harbor seals are true seals because _____

_____

_____

_____

_____

Harbor seals feed on _____

_____

Two interesting facts about harbor seals are _____

_____

_____

_____

_____

_____

_____

_____

_____

_____

GREAT HORNED OWL

Great horned owls can be found throughout the Pacific Northwest. Great horned owls build their nests

_____

They have also been known to steal the nests of

_____

Females lay _____

that hatch in _____

Young great horned owls are ready to leave their nests _____

_____

Like most owls, great horned owls eat_____

_____

Two interesting facts about great horned owls are_____

_____

_____

_____

_____

_____

_____

_____

_____

_____

BALD EAGLE

Bald eagles can be found _____

_____

They eat _____

_____

Their nests can be _____

_____

and are usually built _____

Female bald eagles lay _____

that both parents take turns keeping warm for about _____

_____

Like great horned owls, bald eagles have wingspans that are _____

_____

Two interesting facts about bald eagles are _____

_____

_____

_____

_____

_____

_____

_____

_____

_____

_____

Peregrine Falcon

Peregrine falcons nest in the Pacific Northwest. They usually choose to build their nests _____

_____

_____

_____

Peregrine falcons hunt for _____

_____

In April, female peregrine falcons lay eggs that hatch in about _____

Young peregrine falcons remain in the nest for _____

but stay close to their parents for _____

Two interesting facts about peregrine falcons are _____

_____

_____

_____

_____

_____

_____

_____

_____

_____

_____

DOUBLE-CRESTED CORMORANT

Double-crested cormorants are

commonly seen _____

_____

_____

They choose these spots so they can _____

_____

_____

Both parents work together to build the nest. They also take turns_____

_____

Baby double-crested cormorants wander from their nests _____

to begin _____

Two interesting facts about double-crested cormorants are _____

_____

_____

_____

_____

_____

_____

_____

_____

_____

_____

_____

MOUNTAIN CHICKADEE

Mountain chickadees can be spotted

_____

_____

_____

Female mountain chickadees lay about _____

_____

in a fur lined nest built _____

The eggs hatch in about _____

The young chickadees leave the nest _____

Mountain chickadees are constantly moving in search of _____

_____

_____

Two interesting facts about mountain chickadees are _____

_____

_____

_____

_____

_____

_____

_____

_____

_____

Yellow Warbler

Yellow warblers are tiny birds with

_____

_____

_____

Yellow warblers eat mostly _____

_____

Yellow warblers choose trees to build nests of _____

_____

Females lay _____

The eggs hatch in about _____

Within two weeks, young yellow warblers are _____

_____

Two interesting facts about yellow warblers are _____

_____

_____

_____

_____

_____

_____

_____

_____

_____

✦✦✦✦✦✦ VOCABULARY QUIZ ✦✦✦✦✦✦

WESTWARD EXPANSION
PART IV

DIRECTIONS: Match the vocabulary word on the left with its definition on the right. Put the letter for the definition on the blank next to the vocabulary word it matches. Use each word and definition only once.

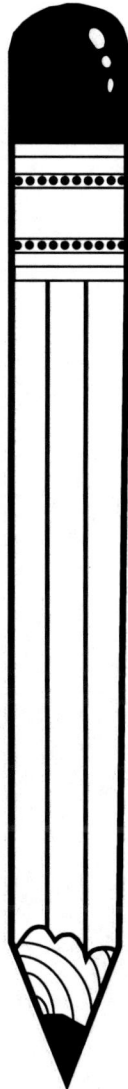

1. _____ addicted

2. _____ typhoid fever

3. _____ centuries

4. _____ tortured

5. _____ small pox

6. _____ ceremonies

7. _____ companions

8. _____ Quakers

9. _____ pursuit

10. _____ competition

11. _____ fertile

12. _____ ammunition

13. _____ Asia

14. _____ conflict

15. _____ Great Plains

16. _____ estuary

17. _____ harbor

A.   permanently settled in another country.

B.   bullets and explosive items used in war.

C.   a battle for victory.

D.   a dangerous disease which causes fever and bumps all over the skin.

E.   one of seven continents in the world. Bounded by Alaska on the northwest, Greenland on the northeast, Florida on the southeast, and Mexico on the southwest.

F.   an illness that causes severe stomach cramps, bleeding, and sometimes even death.

G.   religious or spiritual gatherings.

H.   the world's largest continent with more than half of the Earth's population.

I.   members of a religious group that believed all men were created equal, refused to serve in the military, and would not pay taxes used to support war.

J.   cruelly punished someone by causing severe pain.

K.   types of diseases that spread from one person or animal to another.

L.   problem.

M.   people who travel together.

N.   a region of the northwest United States that includes Washington, Oregon, Idaho, and Montana. It can also include the southwest part of British Columbia, Canada.

O.   periods of 100 years.

18. _____ pioneers

19. _____ headquarters

20. _____ pelts

21. _____ Pacific Northwest

22. _____ inhabited

23. _____ North America

24. _____ mammals

25. _____ infectious

26. _____ omnivores

27. _____ predators

28. _____ immigrated

29. _____ illegally

30. _____ recognition

31. _____ resources

32. _____ ritual

33. _____ shallow

34. _____ talons

35. _____ tides

36. _____ waterfowl

37. _____ peninsula

P.   animals that hunt and eat smaller, more helpless animals.

Q.   lived or settled in a place.

R.   things found in nature that are valuable to humans.

S.   skins and furs of animals.

T.   against the law.

U.   a ceremony performed the same way every time.

V.   animals that eat both meat and plants.

W.   main centers of operation.

X.   not able to stop participating in harmful activities like drinking alcohol or using drugs.

Y.   claws of birds.

Z.   warm-blooded animals that feed their young with milk, have backbones, and are covered with hair.

AA. desire to find.

BB. a large piece of land surrounded by water on three sides.

CC. a grassland region stretching south from Canada to Texas where cattle are raised and wheat is grown.

DD. a hole that is not very deep.

EE. formal approval of an accomplishment.

FF. lower part of a river that flows into the sea.

GG. rich soil that produces a large number of crops.

HH. rises and falls of the ocean.

II. a sheltered area of water deep enough to provide ships a place to anchor.

JJ. birds that swim or live near water, like ducks and geese.

KK. early settlers who prepared the way for others to follow.

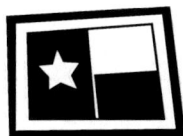

THE TEXAS REVOLUTION

By 1820, news had reached the United States that there was plenty of land and adventure west of the Mississippi River. The United States had become too crowded. Families wanted to own huge areas of land where they could build houses and farms. The stories of brave mountain men and the creation of the Santa Fe Trail made Americans anxious to travel West.

STEPHEN FULLER AUSTIN

Moses Austin, an American businessman, was granted permission from the Spanish government to bring **Catholic** settlers to Texas. Moses died before he could carry out his plans. His son, Stephen F. Austin, set out to complete his father's task.

A few months after his father's death, Stephen Austin learned that Mexico had declared its independence from Spain. At first, the Mexican government refused to honor Moses Austin's agreement with the Spanish government. Stephen Austin traveled to Mexico City and convinced the Mexican government to honor the agreement between his father and Spain.

AMERICANS IN TEXAS

In 1822, Stephen Austin arrived in Texas with 300 Catholic families. They established the Colony of Austin along the Brazos and Colorado rivers. Each Catholic family in the colony received 2,300 acres of free land.

Other American families received the same offer of land from the Mexican government. Soon, thousands of Catholic pioneers traveled to Texas with their black slaves. The settlers planned to use their slaves to help them grow cotton in Texas. Other Americans pretended to be Catholic so they could receive the free land.

STEPHEN F. AUSTIN

By the end of the 1820s, there were more than 20,000 Americans living in Texas. The Mexicans who lived in Texas were against slavery. They were angry with the Americans for bringing their slaves with them.

The Republic of Fredonia (fri•DOHN•ya)

The Americans living in Texas wanted to split from Mexico. They planned to form their own **republic** in Fredonia where they would be free to make their own decisions. A group of 30 American men captured the town of Nacogdoches (nah•coe•DOE•chez). The Mexicans successfully fought back. The Republic of Fredonia failed.

The Mexicans were afraid that they were **outnumbered** by the Americans living in Texas. The Mexican government made some new laws. Americans were no longer permitted to enter Texas. Those who already lived in Texas were not allowed to bring in any more slaves. In addition, the Mexican government required all American settlers in Texas to become Catholic.

In October 1832, under the leadership of Stephen Austin, a group of Americans in Texas wrote a letter to the Mexican government. They wanted the government to change the new laws. The Mexican government refused. Stephen Austin was sent to prison without a trial. Mexico sent General Antonio Lopéz de Santa Anna to Texas. General Santa Anna **enforced** the laws and made sure the Americans stayed **loyal** to Mexico.

The Texas Revolution

The Americans in Texas **rebelled** against General Santa Anna and his rules. In 1835, Stephen Austin was released from prison. He returned to Texas and found the Americans ready to fight for their freedom. A few months later, the Texas Revolution broke out. Austin took command of the Texan Army, but **resigned** after a short period. Instead, he traveled to the United States to borrow money and supplies to fight the war.

The Battle at the Alamo

Early in the Texas Revolution, the Americans took control of the city of San Antonio. They turned the Alamo Mission into a military fort. The flag of Texas was proudly displayed high above the Alamo's walls. General Santa Anna quickly sent Mexican troops to capture the Alamo and regain control of San Antonio.

On February 23, 1836, more than 3,000 Mexican soldiers surrounded the Alamo fort. For 13 days, the Mexican troops blasted the Alamo with cannonballs. The fort's thick **adobe** walls held firm. Inside the fort, 182 Americans were armed with rifles. They promised to fight until victory or death.

On March 6, the Mexicans' cannonballs finally tore a hole in the side of the Alamo. Before the end of the day, all 182 men inside the old mission were dead. Mexican officers reported that the Americans fought to the bitter end. Famous frontiersman Davy Crockett reportedly died

DAVY CROCKETT

while standing on top of a mountain of dead Mexican soldiers that he had personally killed. He swung his rifle wildly and refused to give up. Minutes later, Davy Crockett was also dead.

THE REPUBLIC OF TEXAS

On March 6, 1836, during the Battle at the Alamo, American leaders in Texas held a **convention**. They **adopted** a declaration of independence and declared themselves free of Mexico. Their declaration of independence was much like the one the 13 original colonies had written when they declared their independence from Great Britain. The Americans named their new nation the Republic of Texas. David Burnet was **appointed** president of the Republic of Texas. Sam Houston became the republic's military **commander**.

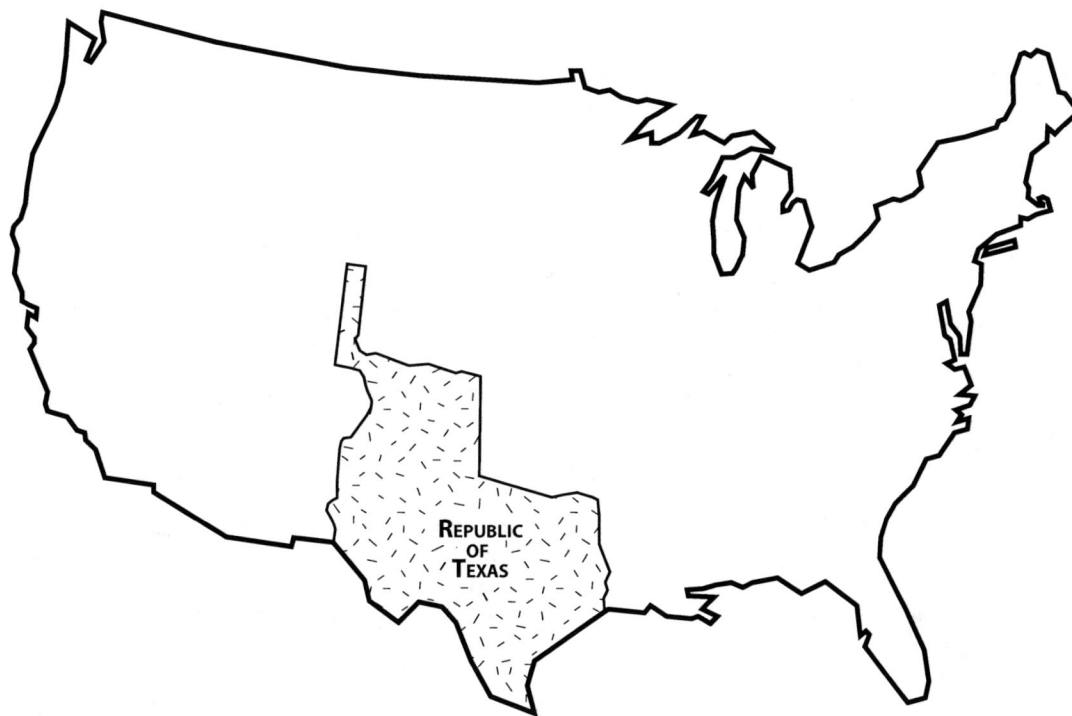

REMEMBERING THE ALAMO

Declaring independence from Mexico did not end the war. General Santa Anna was more determined than ever to defeat the Americans and regain control of Texas. On March 27, in the town of Goliad, General Santa Anna ordered the **execution** of 400 Americans who had surrendered.

The Americans were **outraged** at General Santa Anna's cruelty. They knew then that they had to completely free themselves from Mexico's strong hold. "Remember the Alamo" and "Remember Goliad" became the battle cries of Americans. They would never forget what the Mexicans had done to them.

On April 21, 1836, Sam Houston led a surprise attack on Santa Anna's army. General Santa Anna was captured during the attack. He was forced to surrender. The Texas Revolution was over.

PROBLEMS IN THE REPUBLIC OF TEXAS

Texans elected Sam Houston as the president of the Republic of Texas. Stephen Austin became the secretary of defense. The small nation struggled with Native American wars, **raids** by Mexican forces, and **financial** difficulties.

The Republic of Texas had borrowed money from the United States to fight the Texas Revolution. It had difficulty finding ways to pay the money back.

Texas had plenty of farm land for growing crops and making money, but most of the land was inhabited by Native Americans. The Native Americans weren't willing to give up their fertile land.

TEXAS JOINS THE UNITED STATES

Texans wanted to become part of the United States. The problem was, the Republic of Texas allowed slavery. The Northern states did not want Texas to join the Union. Despite this, Texas was admitted as the 28th state on December 29, 1845. Texans elected Sam Houston as the state's first governor. Texans were allowed to own slaves, but the state had to pay back all of its debt to the United States. As American settlers moved into Texas, the Native Americans were forced to sign treaties with the United States government and move to the Indian Territory.

TEXAS FLAG

THE INDIAN TERRITORY

In 1830, the Indian Territory had been created out of land in the present-day states of Oklahoma, Kansas, Nebraska, and the Dakotas. Native Americans in the Southeast region of the United States had already been forced to give up their land and move to the Indian Territory.

THE TRAIL OF TEARS

From 1830 to 1842, thousands of Native Americans from 30 different tribes had been moved to the Indian Territory. Not all of them agreed to go peacefully. Those who refused to go were dragged from their homes in chains.

Almost half of the Native Americans died along what became known as the "Trail of Tears." Disease, starvation, and freezing temperatures along the 1,000-mile journey took the lives of entire families. The United States government had promised to provide food and water along the route. Most of the time the supplies did not arrive on time, or food sat out on the trail and spoiled.

As more Americans settled west of the Mississippi River in places like Texas, the United States government forced the Native Americans to sign treaties and join the other Native American tribes living in the Indian Territory.

THE TEXAS REVOLUTION

Directions: Read each question carefully. Darken the circle for the correct answer.

---

1 When Stephen Austin's Catholic settlers arrived in Texas, they received –

   A free land

   B a parade

   C beaver furs

   D Spanish and Native American gifts

2 The Mexicans living in Texas were angry with the Americans because –

   F the Americans settled wherever they pleased

   G the Americans brought their slaves with them

   H the Americans were unfriendly to the Native Americans

   J the Americans planted cotton

3 After the Republic of Fredonia failed, the Mexican government required all American settlers in Texas to –

   A go to prison

   B leave Texas

   C become Catholic

   D purchase more slaves

4 What did Stephen Austin do during the Texas Revolution?

   F He fought in the Battle at the Alamo.

   G He traveled to the United States to borrow money and supplies.

   H He killed Davy Crockett.

   J He stayed in prison.

5 After the Battle at the Alamo, what did General Santa Anna do to show the Americans that he was in control?

   A He became the president of Mexico.

   B He ordered the execution of 400 Americans.

   C He killed Stephen Austin.

   D He destroyed the Alamo Mission.

6 All of the following were problems in the Republic of Texas except –

   F Native American wars

   G Mexican raids

   H financial difficulties

   J plenty of fertile farm land

7 During the Trail of Tears, what happened to Native Americans who refused to leave their homes?

   A They were permitted to stay.

   B They were dragged from their homes in chains.

   C They were sent to live in Mexico.

   D They were given a few extra days to change their minds and leave their homes peacefully.

READING

Answers

1 Ⓐ Ⓑ Ⓒ Ⓓ   5 Ⓐ Ⓑ Ⓒ Ⓓ
2 Ⓕ Ⓖ Ⓗ Ⓙ   6 Ⓕ Ⓖ Ⓗ Ⓙ
3 Ⓐ Ⓑ Ⓒ Ⓓ   7 Ⓐ Ⓑ Ⓒ Ⓓ
4 Ⓕ Ⓖ Ⓗ Ⓙ

Famous People: Andrew Jackson

On March 15, 1767, Andrew Jackson was born in a log cabin near the border of present-day North and South Carolina. He was the son of poor immigrants from Ireland. Andrew's father died a few months after Andrew was born. As a child, Andrew was known for his quick temper and willingness to fight anybody at anytime. He was involved in so many fights that he had bullets near his lungs and heart that couldn't be removed. As an adult, he killed a man who made rude comments toward his wife.

Revolutionary War Soldier

During the Revolutionary War, when British troops **invaded** South Carolina, 13 year old Andrew Jackson joined the Continental Army. In 1781, during a battle, Andrew and his brother were captured and thrown into prison. Both boys caught small pox while in prison. Andrew survived, but his brother died of the disease. A short time after Andrew was released from prison, his mother died. Andrew Jackson was only 14 years old. He was left alone to take care of himself.

Government Leader

After the Revolutionary War, Andrew became a lawyer and moved to the present-day state of Tennessee. In 1788, he was appointed **attorney general** of Tennessee. Jackson's job as attorney general was to make sure that the residents of Tennessee paid their taxes and obeyed the laws. He was very **harsh** with criminals and sent many people to jail.

Andrew Jackson held other government positions during the early years of our nation. He served as a **delegate** to the state constitutional convention and helped Tennessee become a state. In 1796, Jackson was elected to Congress. Two years later, he was elected to Tennessee's **Supreme Court**.

ANDREW JACKSON

Jackson and his wife Rachel bought a farm and built the first general store in Gallatin, Tennessee. By 1804, they were growing cotton on their 1,000-acre plantation. At one point, Andrew and his wife owned more than 100 black slaves.

Old Hickory

During his years in Congress, Andrew Jackson disagreed with President George Washington's friendly treatment of Native Americans. Jackson felt that the Native Americans should be forced from their land so the United States could grow. During the War of 1812, Jackson quickly volunteered to fight against Great Britain and its Native American allies. He earned the nickname "Old Hickory" because his soldiers said he was as tough as an old hickory tree.

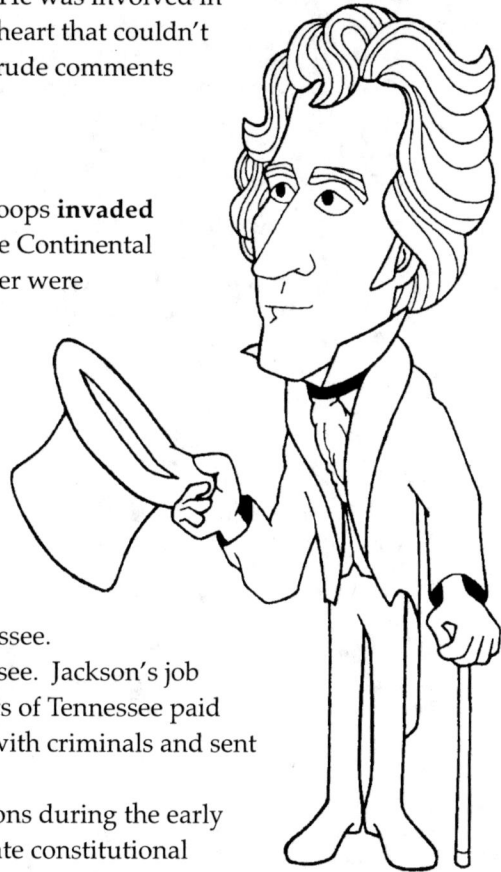

GENERAL JACKSON

Andrew Jackson led several battles against Native Americans during the War of 1812. The Battle of Horseshoe Bend resulted in the deaths of 800 Native Americans of the Creek tribe. He was **promoted** to General Jackson after that battle. General Jackson became a hero when he captured the city of New Orleans. His troops killed or wounded more than 1,500 Native Americans and British soldiers.

After the War of 1812, General Jackson continued to command the Southern Army. In December 1817, he was ordered to lead his troops to the Florida-Georgia border. Native Americans of the Creek and Seminole (SEM•uh•nol) tribes had been raiding American settlements along the border. General Jackson and his soldiers defeated the Native Americans and chased them into Spanish-controlled Florida.

PRESIDENT JACKSON

In 1829, at the age of 61, Andrew Jackson was elected as the seventh president of the United States. His wife Rachel died two weeks after the election.

During his two terms as president, President Jackson tried to represent the "common man." He was the first president born in a log cabin to parents who weren't wealthy. He wanted a strong federal government and voted against laws that gave more power to individual states.

THE INDIAN REMOVAL ACT

SEMINOLE WARRIOR

President Jackson did not think that Native Americans and white settlers could live together in the same states. He was in favor of moving the Native Americans to the Indian Territory in the present-day states of Oklahoma, Kansas, Nebraska, and the Dakotas. Individual states passed laws that allowed them to force Native Americans from their land. Although President Jackson was against giving states so much power, he did not **interfere** with the states' laws when they dealt with the treatment of Native Americans.

In 1830, with President Jackson's support, Congress passed the Indian Removal Act. Native Americans east of the Mississippi River were required to move to the Indian Territory. Thousands of Native Americans were forced from their homes to make room for white settlers.

JACKSON'S LATER YEARS

Andrew Jackson was a very sickly president. He suffered from **chronic** headaches and stomach pains. He frequently coughed up blood because of a bullet that was still in his lung. After his presidency, Jackson retired to Nashville, Tennessee. He died on June 8, 1945, at the age of 78. Except for a few personal items, Andrew Jackson left everything to his adopted son, Andrew Jackson, Jr.

FAMOUS PEOPLE: ANDREW JACKSON

Directions: Use the selection about Andrew Jackson to answer these questions. Circle the answers to questions 1 and 2. Write your answers on the lines provided for questions 3-6.

1 After reading the first paragraph about Andrew Jackson, you learn that –

   A he was a very quiet child

   B he was born in South Dakota

   C his parents were wealthy

   D he killed a man

2 In 1796, Andrew Jackson was elected to Congress. In 1829, he was elected as president. How many years passed between these two important events?

   A 43

   B 33

   C 76

   D 24

3 As a child, Andrew Jackson was known for his quick temper and willingness to fight anybody at anytime. Talk to someone who knows you very well. How does that person describe you?

_____

_____

Do you agree with this description? Explain. _____

_____

4 Describe one way that Andrew Jackson's quick temper and willingness to fight hurt him when he became an adult.

_____

_____

5 Describe one way that Andrew Jackson's quick temper and willingness to fight helped him when he became an adult.

_____

_____

6 Look again at the way someone described you in Number 3. Do you think that will hurt you or help you when you become an adult? Explain.

_____

_____

_____

꧁꧁꧁꧁꧁꧁꧁ VOCABULARY QUIZ ꧁꧁꧁꧁꧁꧁꧁
WESTWARD EXPANSION
PART V

DIRECTIONS: Match the vocabulary word on the left with its definition on the right. Put the letter for the definition on the blank next to the vocabulary word it matches. Use each word and definition only once.

1. _____ annual

2. _____ interfere

3. _____ artifacts

4. _____ harsh

5. _____ financial

6. _____ baleen

7. _____ barbed

8. _____ execution

9. _____ enforced

10. _____ delegate

11. _____ canine

12. _____ circumvent

13. _____ climate

14. _____ convention

15. _____ commander

16. _____ chronic

17. _____ Continental Army

A. sharp pointed hooks.

B. protected from injury or ruin so more can be learned.

C. carried out an order to kill someone.

D. constant pain over a long period of time.

E. pointed, cone-shaped teeth.

F. the highest law officer of the state.

G. very uncomfortable conditions.

H. family members who come after one has died.

I. to hunt another animal for food.

J. member of a Christian church who traces his or her history back to the twelve apostles.

K. went long periods without eating.

L. a part of a country having a government of its own.

M. the bendable substance taken from the upper jaw of certain whales.

N. an event that takes place once a year.

O. to keep safe from danger, attack, or harm.

P. a meeting where important decisions are made.

18. _____ defend

19. _____ Catholic

20. _____ descendants

21. _____ fasted

22. _____ attorney general

23. _____ generosity

24. _____ harpoon

25. _____ appointed

26. _____ adopted

27. _____ herbivores

28. _____ invaded

29. _____ inactive

30. _____ influence

31. _____ loyal

32. _____ mountainous

33. _____ poverty

34. _____ preserved

35. _____ adobe

36. _____ prey

37. _____ province

Q. a heavy clay used for making bricks.

R. required someone to obey the rules.

S. to go around.

T. the average condition of weather over a period of years.

U. American troops that fought against Great Britain during the Revolutionary War.

V. entered an area and took it over by force.

W. objects and tools used by early humans for eating, cooking, and hunting.

X. faithful.

Y. extremely poor living conditions.

Z. a leader in charge of a military unit.

AA. animals that feed mainly on plants.

BB. chosen or selected.

CC. having the power to affect others' actions and behaviors.

DD. giving freely of time or money.

EE. part of a business that has to do with money.

FF. a person sent with power to represent others.

GG. a place that has many mountains.

HH. long periods with no movement.

II. accepted and put into action.

JJ. bother or disturb by giving advice when it isn't wanted.

KK. a spear with hooks on it used for hunting whales and large fish.

THE OREGON TRAIL

By the 1840s, many things had changed in the United States. In less than 70 years as a nation, the United States had organized a strong government, more than doubled its size with the Louisiana Purchase, moved thousands of Native Americans to the Indian Territory, and **acquired** the state of Texas.

The profitable fur trade had been expanded into the Pacific Northwest. News of fertile land and wide open spaces in Oregon Country made Americans want to travel West.

AMERICAN MISSIONARIES

Some of the first Americans to travel to the Pacific Northwest were not families searching for fertile farm land. They were **missionaries**. The trip was dangerous, but the missionaries were willing to risk their lives to help the area's Native Americans.

In March 1836, American doctor Marcus Whitman and missionary Henry Spalding loaded their supplies in two large wagons. They left St. Louis and headed toward Oregon Country. Dr. Whitman and Henry Spalding took their wives, Narcissa Whitman and Eliza Spalding, and a group of 70 fur traders.

As they traveled, the Whitmans and Spaldings depended upon the hunters in their party to supply them with buffalo meat. They used the milk and beef from 15 cows they brought with them on their journey. The heavy wagons were not able to cross the Rocky Mountains. They were forced to leave their wagons and most of their supplies and cross the mountains on mules.

ARRIVING IN OREGON COUNTRY

Six months after leaving St. Louis, the Whitmans and Spaldings reached Oregon Country. Narcissa and Eliza were the first white women to cross the **Continental Divide**. The Whitmans built a mission in present-day Washington. They planned to teach the Cayuse (kie•YOOS) people about farming and **Christianity**. The Spaldings traveled on to Idaho. They **founded** a mission among the Nez Percé (nay•pair•SAY) people.

NARCISSA WHITMAN

THE CAYUSE MISSION

The Cayuse were hunters, not farmers. They were very **devoted** to their own religion. They did not want to learn about Christianity. In 1842, Marcus Whitman left the mission and returned with 900 new settlers. Someone in the group unknowingly brought measles to the mission. The disease spread quickly and killed 14 Cayuse children.

The Cayuse blamed the missionaries for bringing the disease that killed their children. They thought the missionaries were trying to poison them. They also hated the missionaries for taking their land. In 1847, the Cayuse killed the Whitmans and 12 other people who lived at the mission. They set fire to the mission buildings and kidnapped the white women and children. The Americans fought back and burned the Cayuse village. The Cayuse people were defeated and forced to live on a **reservation** in Washington.

THE OREGON TRAIL

Although the Whitmans failed as missionaries, they proved that people could successfully travel to the West. The Whitmans led the way for others wishing to go to Oregon Country. For the next 20 years, Americans traveled on what became known as the Oregon Trail. Those who were able to survive the journey were rewarded with fertile soil and open spaces.

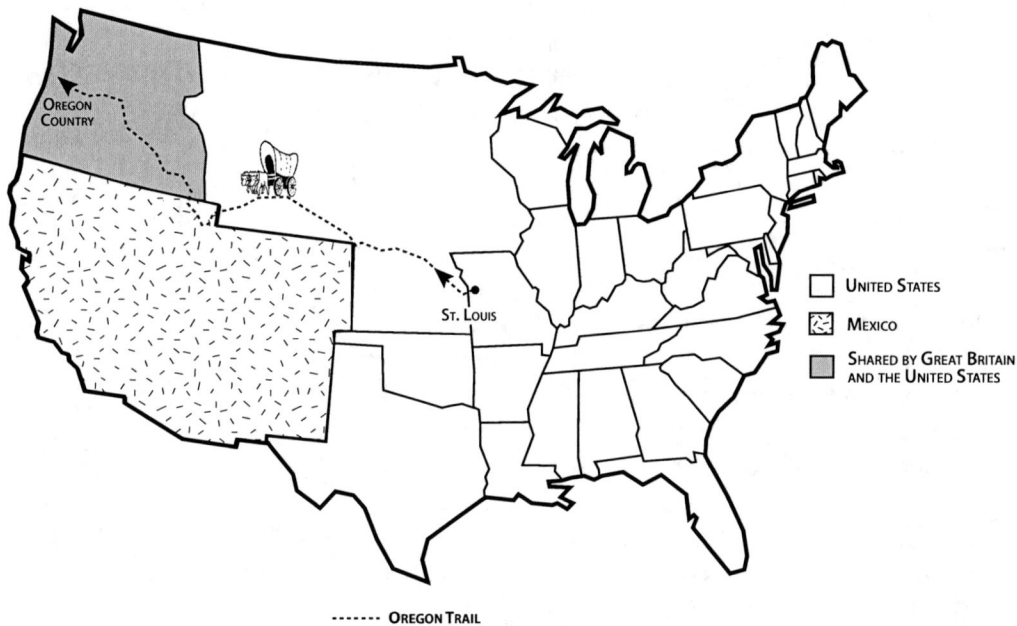

------- OREGON TRAIL

FAST FACTS

- The most popular animals for pulling wagons over the Oregon Trail were oxen. They were cheaper, stronger, and easier to work with than horses or mules. Mules cost $75.00 each. An oxen could be purchased for $25.00.
- Oxen were also less likely to be stolen by Native Americans on the journey. They made good farm animals once the pioneers reached the end of the trail.

LIFE ON THE OREGON TRAIL

The Oregon Trail stretched for 2,000 miles from St. Louis to the Columbia River in Oregon Country. The journey was dangerous. Pioneers loaded all of their possessions into small covered wagons. For safety, several families traveled together. They formed one long wagon train. Oxen pulled the wagons. Horses and cattle walked along behind.

The wagon trains moved very slowly. They traveled just 12 to 15 miles each day. It took four to six months for pioneers to travel from Missouri to Oregon Country. Today, that same journey takes about three days by car or six hours by airplane.

Many families died from illness, starvation, and Native American attacks along the Oregon Trail. There were hot and dusty weeks of walking through deserts under the burning sun. Other times it rained and the wagons got stuck in the mud. There were accidents and illnesses, but no hospitals along the trail. Native American attacks were frequent. At night, the wagons formed a large circle for protection from wild animals and hostile Native Americans.

Crossing rivers was very difficult. There were no bridges. The travelers had to stop and build wooden rafts to carry their wagons. Many of the animals drowned trying to swim across the rivers.

CROSSING THE MOUNTAINS

One of the most difficult parts of the journey was crossing the Rocky Mountains and the **Sierra Nevada**. It was hard enough to pass through these steep mountains and rugged cliffs when the weather was warm. Trees had to be chopped down. Sometimes there was no grass for the animals to eat.

During the winter months, the journey was even more dangerous. The oxen could not pull the wagons over the steep mountains. The wagons had to be emptied of personal belongings. Sometimes the wagons had to be taken apart so they could be lowered down the steep mountains.

This part of the trip claimed many lives. Gravestones marked the trail. The mountains were littered with furniture, pieces of wagons, and skeletons of dead animals.

THE DONNER PARTY

The Donner Party was one of the most famous groups to cross the Oregon Trail. Instead of traveling on one of the tested trails, the Donner Party took a shorter route through eastern Utah. Arguing over which direction to take cost the group weeks of valuable time. They began crossing the dangerous Sierra Nevada in late October. Within a week they were trapped in the heavy snow.

The group quickly ran out of food. Half their party froze or starved to death. Some of the survivors even ate the flesh of those who had died. Only 47 of the original 87 members lived long enough to be rescued. After hearing about the Donner Party, other pioneer families made sure they left early in the spring and stayed on the trail.

THE OLD SPANISH TRAIL

The Oregon Trail wasn't the only route West. You have already read how the Santa Fe Trail led the mountain men from Missouri to Santa Fe, New Mexico. In 1829, Mexican explorer Jose Antonio Armijo (ar•MEE•ho) gathered a group of 60 men to explore the West and create a new trade route from Santa Fe to California. Armijo's route became known as the Old Spanish Trail.

THE CALIFORNIA TRAIL

In 1841, American pioneer John Bidwell left Missouri and traveled north along the Oregon Trail. After reaching present-day Idaho, Bidwell and his group left the Oregon Trail and traveled south through Utah and Nevada. He led the first group of pioneers overland into Sacramento along what became known as the California Trail.

THE GILA TRAIL

In 1846, the United States government sent Captain Philip Cooke to Santa Fe, New Mexico. Captain Cooke and his group of **Mormon** soldiers were instructed to find a route from Santa Fe to San Diego, California. The route, which was first traveled by Native Americans and Arizona missionaries, became known as the Gila Trail. It was 1,000 miles long and stretched through the Arizona desert, along the banks of the Colorado River, and into the steep mountains of California.

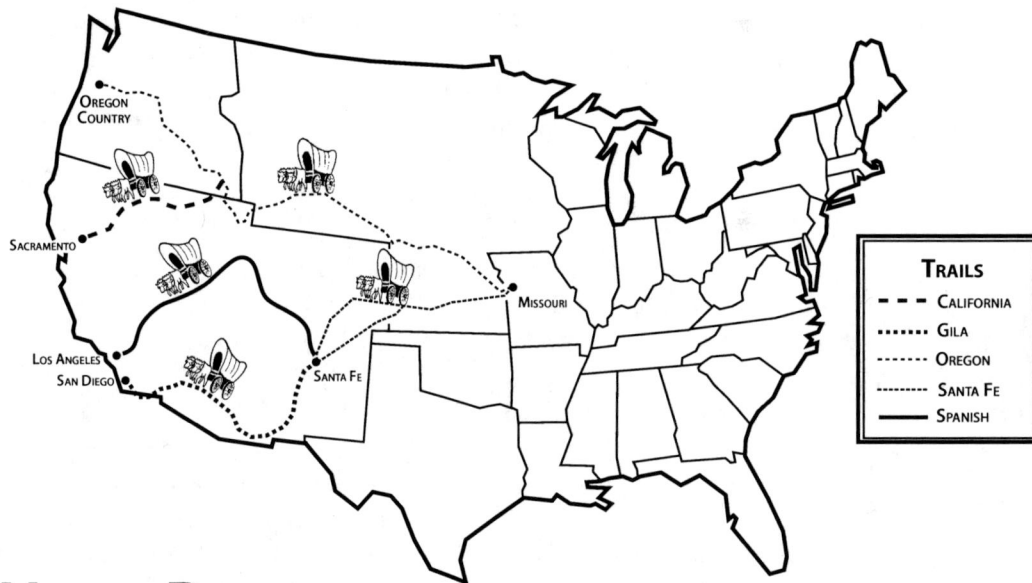

MANIFEST DESTINY

As Americans followed the trails into the West, the Mexican government became fearful that the United States would try to take control of Mexico's territory. Mexico had good reason to be worried. The United States was interested in Mexico's land, especially the land in California.

In fact, Americans came up with the phrase "Manifest Destiny" which meant it was God's will for the United States to extend from the Atlantic to the Pacific oceans. The trails leading West put the United States one step closer to its "Manifest Destiny."

Name _____

⟨⟩⟨⟩⟨⟩⟨⟩⟨⟩ THE OREGON TRAIL ⟨⟩⟨⟩⟨⟩⟨⟩⟨⟩

Directions: Read each question carefully. Darken the circle for the correct answer.

---

1 **Why did missionaries want to risk their lives traveling to Oregon Country?**

   A They wanted to own land.

   B They wanted to help the Native Americans.

   C They wanted to become farmers.

   D They wanted to see if horses and cows could make it across the Rocky Mountains.

2 **The Cayuse Mission was unsuccessful for all of the following reasons except –**

   F the Cayuse were devoted to their own religion

   G the Cayuse hated the missionaries for taking their land

   H the Cayuse welcomed the help from the missionaries

   J the Cayuse blamed the missionaries for bringing a disease that killed their children

3 **What were the most popular animals for pulling wagons across the Oregon Trail?**

   A Mules

   B Horses

   C Buffalo

   D Oxen

4 **Why was crossing the Sierra Nevada one of the most dangerous parts of the Oregon Trail?**

   F The flat ground made it difficult to walk for long periods.

   G There was too much grass in the Sierra Nevada to pull the wagons through.

   H It was difficult to pull the wagons over the steep mountains.

   J It was very hot in the Sierra Nevada.

5 **What was the biggest mistake made by the Donner Party?**

   A They waited too long to cross the Sierra Nevada and got trapped in heavy snow.

   B Their group was too large.

   C They took too much food with them.

   D They refused to take a shorter route which would have saved them valuable time.

6 **After studying the map of famous trails you learn that –**

   F the Spanish Trail was south of the Gila Trail

   G the California Trail was north of the Oregon Trail

   H the Gila Trail ended in Sacramento

   J the Spanish Trail ended in Los Angeles

Answers   READING

1 Ⓐ Ⓑ Ⓒ Ⓓ   4 Ⓕ Ⓖ Ⓗ Ⓙ

2 Ⓕ Ⓖ Ⓗ Ⓙ   5 Ⓐ Ⓑ Ⓒ Ⓓ

3 Ⓐ Ⓑ Ⓒ Ⓓ   6 Ⓕ Ⓖ Ⓗ Ⓙ

FAMOUS PEOPLE: GEORGE WASHINGTON BUSH

George Washington Bush was born in Pennsylvania. Historians aren't sure of his exact birth date, but most agree it was around 1779. As an only child, George was raised as a Quaker and went to school in Philadelphia. His parents were **servants** who worked in the home of a wealthy English **merchant**. When the merchant died, he left his fortune to the Bush family.

As an adult, George Washington Bush fought in the War of 1812. After the war, he worked as an explorer and a fur trapper. He spent several years in Oregon Country working for John McLoughlin's Hudson's Bay Company.

LIFE IN MISSOURI

In 1830, George traveled to Missouri where he met and married Isabella, the daughter of a preacher. The couple had six sons. In Missouri, the Bush family made a lot of money farming and raising cattle. Isabella, a white woman, was a nurse.

Missouri was a slave state during the 1830s. Even though George was a free black man, Missouri did not offer him the same rights and freedoms as a white citizen. George and Isabella wanted to raise their sons in a place that was free from **discrimination**. They chose Oregon Country.

OREGON COUNTRY

In 1844, the Bush family joined several white families and left Missouri. After making the dangerous six month journey along the Oregon Trail, the Bush family was turned away from the Willamette Valley in present-day Oregon because of George's skin color. The settlers in the Willamette Valley had voted to keep blacks out.

George Washington Bush got permission from the Hudson's Bay Company for his entire party to settle in an area of Oregon Country that was shared by the United States and Great Britain.

GEORGE WASHINGTON BUSH

Bush's group chose 640 acres of fertile land that became known as Bush Prairie. The Bush family used seeds they had brought and began farming. Through hard work, their farm became the most successful in the area. Within a few years, Bush and his white friends had built a **sawmill** and a **gristmill**.

THE OREGON TERRITORY

George Bush was friendly with the Native Americans. The Nisqually tribe taught the newcomers how to find oysters, dig for clams, and fish for salmon in the area's rivers. The entire Bush family learned the Nisqually language. When **epidemic** diseases swept the region, George Bush helped treat the sick Native Americans.

Bush was also a friend to new pioneers, black and white, who often arrived sick and starving from their journeys along the Oregon Trail.

In 1846, the land in present-day Washington, including Bush Prairie, became part of the United States. Two years later, the United States created the Oregon Territory. The Oregon Territory included the present-day states of Washington, Oregon, Idaho, and parts of Montana and Wyoming.

1848

☐ Oregon Territory

Laws in the Oregon Territory did not allow African Americans to own property. Fortunately, George Washington Bush's generosity to others paid off. The United States government allowed the Bush family to keep its land.

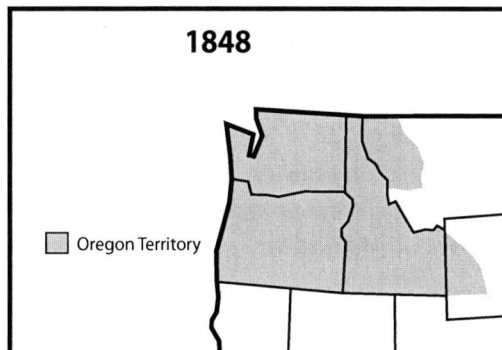

OREGON TERRITORY'S EXCLUSION LAWS

It was very difficult for other black pioneers to follow George Washington Bush's example and settle in the Pacific Northwest. Slavery was illegal in the Oregon Territory. Still, many white pioneers brought their black slaves with them across the Oregon Trail. The white residents wrote "**exclusion** laws" to keep African Americans from living in the Oregon Territory. Oregon's laws required white slave owners to free their black slaves within three years.

Free blacks were not permitted to settle in the Oregon Territory and had to leave the area within three years of being set free. Those who broke the law and stayed were not permitted to own property or vote. They couldn't find jobs and were arrested if caught walking through white neighborhoods. As a result, few African Americans were part of the Pacific Northwest's earliest history.

FAST FACTS	• George Washington Bush died on April 5, 1863. He is the only **veteran** of the War of 1812 buried in Thurston County, Washington. • Five of George Washington Bush's sons were born in Missouri. The sixth was born on the Bush Prairie. His middle name was Nisqually, in honor of the Native Americans who helped the Bush family in Oregon Country. • Bush's oldest son, William Owen Bush, was elected twice to the Washington State **Legislature**. In 1890, he introduced the bill that created Washington State University.

FAMOUS PEOPLE: GEORGE WASHINGTON BUSH

Directions: Use the selection about George Washington Bush to answer these questions. Circle the answers to questions 1 and 2. Write your answers on the lines provided for questions 3-5.

1 After reading about George Washington Bush, you learn that –

    A he married a black woman

    B he refused to live near white people

    C his skin color kept him from living wherever he wanted

    D he was not a very successful farmer

2 George Washington Bush was born in 1779 and died in 1863. How old was he when he died?

    A 57

    B 84

    C 16

    D 94

3 George Washington Bush was discriminated against because of the color of his skin. Have you ever been discriminated against? Explain how it made you feel. If you have never been discriminated against, describe how you would feel if your family was forced to leave your neighborhood because you were different in some way.

_____

_____

_____

4 Give two examples of positive things George Washington Bush did in his life.

    a. _____

_____

    b. _____

_____

5 If George Washington Bush was alive today, do you think he would be proud of the way black and white Americans treat each other? Give reasons for your answer.

_____

_____

_____

_____

THE MEXICAN WAR

There are only two ways for a country to gain new territory: buy it like the United States did with the Louisiana Purchase, or win it in a war. By 1846, Americans had been traveling along the Oregon and Santa Fe trails for more than 20 years. The United States became interested in taking control of Mexico's land in the West.

Remember, Americans came up with the phrase "Manifest Destiny." They believed it was God's will for the United States to extend from the Atlantic to the Pacific oceans.

The United States was especially interested in California. The Mexican government refused to sell California to the United States.

Mexico and the United States also argued over boundaries. The two countries could not agree on the southern boundary of Texas. It seemed that the only way to gain more land and settle the boundary dispute was to go to war. In 1846, the United States declared war on Mexico.

Though Mexico was better prepared for the war, the American troops had stronger leaders and **superior** equipment. From 1846 to 1847, the United States won almost every battle fought. American armies were led by famous men like Colonel Stephen Kearney, Kit Carson, John C. Frémont, Captain Philip Cooke, and Pauline Weaver. They marched in and easily took over Santa Fe, Los Angeles, Tucson, and other Mexican territories.

A PLAN FOR PEACE

Within a short time, Mexico had lost four times as many men in battle than the United States. In the spring of 1847, President James Polk sent Nicholas P. Trist to discuss a peace treaty with Mexico. President Polk hoped that this would end the war.

The president of Mexico refused to talk about peace with the United States. The Mexican War continued. In August, the United States Army marched into Mexico City and captured Mexico's capital. Mexico's president stepped down from power. A new government took control in Mexico. The new leaders feared that if they didn't sign the peace treaty with the United States, the war would continue. More Mexican land and lives would be lost.

THE TREATY OF GUADALUPE-HIDALGO

On February 2, 1848, a peace treaty was signed between Mexico and the United States in the Mexican village of Guadalupe-Hidalgo. In this agreement, Mexico accepted the Rio Grande River as the southwestern boundary of Texas. Mexico also gave the United States its entire region of New Mexico. This included the northern half of Arizona and the land that one day became the states of California, Colorado, Nevada, New Mexico, Utah, and Wyoming. In return, the United States paid Mexico 15 million dollars. Mexicans who already lived in these areas were permitted to remain and become United States citizens.

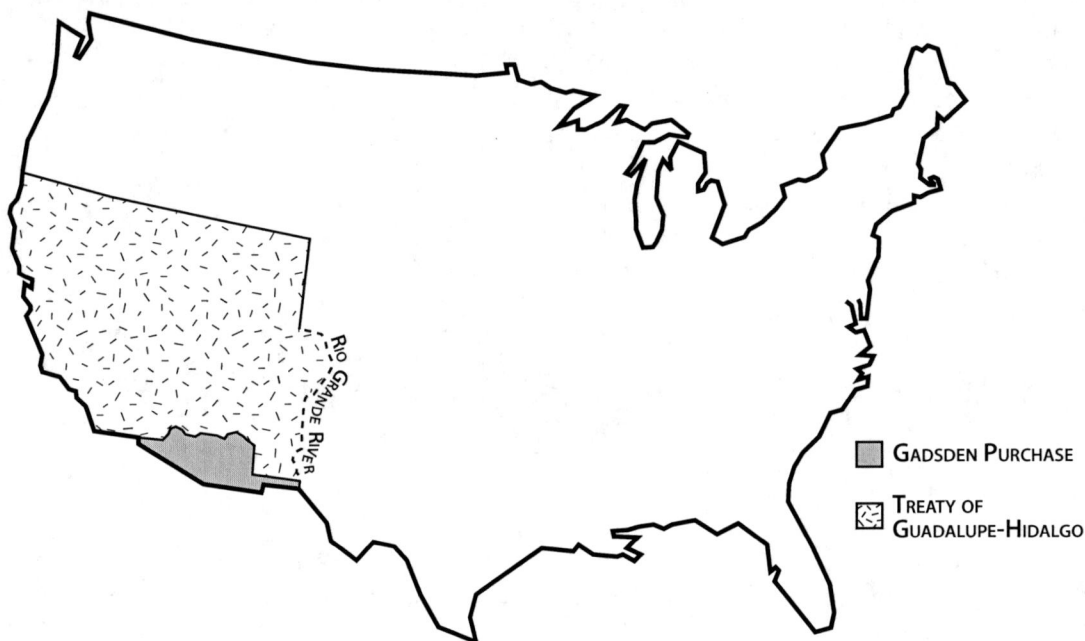

■ GADSDEN PURCHASE

▨ TREATY OF GUADALUPE-HIDALGO

THE GADSDEN PURCHASE

In 1853, Mexico sold more land to the United States. This was known as the Gadsden Purchase. The Gadsden Purchase added 29,000 square miles of land to the United States and cost the United States 10 million dollars. The land included the southern half of Arizona and part of the present-day state of New Mexico. The southwest boundary of the United States was complete.

FAST FACTS

- During the Mexican War, the first stamps issued by the United States Post Office went on sale. Two different stamps could be purchased.
- For letters traveling under 300 miles, the 5¢ stamp picturing Benjamin Franklin was used. For letters traveling over 300 miles, the 10¢ stamp featuring George Washington was used.

Name _____

◈◈◈◈◈ THE MEXICAN WAR ◈◈◈◈◈

Directions: Read each question carefully. Darken the circle for the correct answer.

1 After reading the first few paragraphs about the Mexican War, you get the idea that –

A the United States was not interested in taking control of Mexico's land

B Mexico wanted to sell California

C the United States planned to steal Mexico's land

D Mexico wanted to keep California for itself

2 In the fifth paragraph, what does the word <u>superior</u> mean?

F less

G first

H better

J last

3 Why did Mexico's leaders finally decide to sign a peace treaty with the United States?

A Mexico's leaders felt the United States deserved to win the war.

B Mexico's leaders wanted to continue fighting the United States.

C Mexico's leaders didn't want to lose any more land or lives.

D Mexico's leaders planned to steal the land back from the United States.

4 Why was the peace treaty named the Treaty of Guadalupe-Hidalgo?

F It was signed in the village of Guadalupe-Hidalgo.

G It was named after Mexican soldiers Guadalupe and Hidalgo.

H It was named after President Guadalupe-Hidalgo.

J It was signed on the Mexican holiday Guadalupe-Hidalgo Day.

5 The Treaty of Guadalupe-Hidalgo included all of these future states <u>except</u> –

A California

B North Dakota

C Utah

D New Mexico

6 What can you learn from studying the map of the Guadalupe-Hidalgo Treaty and the Gadsden Purchase?

F The Rio Grande River is south of the Gadsden Purchase.

G The area of land bought in the Gadsden Purchase is larger than the land given in the Treaty of Guadalupe-Hidalgo.

H The Gadsden Purchase is north of the Rio Grande River.

J The Rio Grande River forms the eastern boundaries of the Treaty of Guadalupe-Hidalgo and the Gadsden Purchase.

7 Which of these statements about the Gadsden Purchase is <u>true</u>?

A It added 29,000 square miles of land to the United States.

B The Gadsden Purchase cost the United States 15 million dollars.

C The Gadsden Purchase included the northern half of Arizona.

D The land from the Gadsden Purchase became the California Territory.

READING

Answers

1 Ⓐ Ⓑ Ⓒ Ⓓ   5 Ⓐ Ⓑ Ⓒ Ⓓ
2 Ⓕ Ⓖ Ⓗ Ⓙ   6 Ⓕ Ⓖ Ⓗ Ⓙ
3 Ⓐ Ⓑ Ⓒ Ⓓ   7 Ⓐ Ⓑ Ⓒ Ⓓ
4 Ⓕ Ⓖ Ⓗ Ⓙ

Famous People: John C. Frémont and Kit Carson

John Charles Frémont was born in Georgia on January 21, 1813. He grew up to be an American military officer, explorer, governor, and **senator**.

During the 1830s, Frémont led several expeditions through the West and beyond. From 1838 to 1839, he explored the lands between the Mississippi and Missouri rivers. In 1841, he mapped part of the Des Moines (duh•MOIN) River in present-day Idaho.

Kit Carson

Christopher "Kit" Carson was born on December 24, 1809, in Kentucky. The Carson family moved to Missouri a year after Kit was born. When Kit was seven years old, his father was killed by a falling tree.

Kit dropped out of school to hunt and work on his family's farm. As a result, he never learned to read or write. At the age of 16, Kit secretly joined a group that was headed to Santa Fe, New Mexico. His job was to take care of the horses, mules, and oxen.

In New Mexico, Kit was taught the skills of trapping and trading. He also learned how to speak Spanish and several Native American languages. During the 1830s, Carson used the skills he learned to trap and trade beaver pelts throughout the present-day states of Colorado, Utah, Wyoming, Idaho, and Montana. By 1840, Kit Carson knew the Santa Fe and Oregon trails better than any mountain man.

Frémont and Carson Expeditions

In 1842, John C. Frémont and Kit Carson met for the first time. Frémont was preparing to lead an expedition across the Oregon Trail through the Rocky Mountains and into eastern Wyoming. He planned to find a river that he hoped connected the Great Lakes to the Pacific Ocean. Frémont hired Kit Carson to be his guide. While the pair did not find a connection between the Great Lakes and the Pacific Ocean, the five month journey was considered a success. Frémont's report of fur bearing animals and fertile land made other Americans want to travel West.

From 1842 to 1846, Frémont and Carson led wagon trains over the Oregon Trail. During one of their winter journeys, they got caught in the deep snow of the Sierra Nevada and almost starved to death. They reported that their mules ate one another's tails and the leather saddles to stay alive.

During their expeditions, the pair made many of the West's first maps. The Carson River in present-day Nevada was discovered and named after Kit Carson. Pyramid Lake, also in Nevada, was named because of its giant pyramid shaped rock **formation**.

Carson and Frémont became the first Americans to see Lake Tahoe. Frémont climbed the second highest peak in the Wind River Mountains, known today as Frémont Peak. He also made maps of many volcanoes, including Washington's Mount St. Helens.

THE GREAT BASIN

During one of their expeditions, Frémont noticed that many of the rivers in the West did not flow into the sea. Instead, they either dried up or emptied into **inland** lakes. Frémont thought that the land between the Sierra Nevada Mountain Range and the Rocky Mountains looked like a giant bowl or **basin** filled with water. The Great Basin is the name still used today to describe this land.

THE MEXICAN WAR

During the Mexican War, Frémont and Carson joined forces with naval commander Robert Stockton and took control of Los Angeles without a fight from Mexican troops. After the victory, John C. Frémont was appointed governor of the California Territory.

For the next two years, Kit Carson was sent back and forth from California to Washington to deliver messages. Each 2,600 mile journey was completed not by plane, train, or car, but on horseback.

In 1848, Frémont left California and led an expedition to map the best places for a railroad that would run from the Rio Grande River to California. While he was away, gold was discovered on his California **estate**. Frémont instantly became a very wealthy man. In 1850, California became a state. John C. Frémont returned to California and became one of the state's first senators.

THE CIVIL WAR

Kit Carson and John C. Frémont both fought for the **Union Army** during the **Civil War**. Carson spent most of his time battling hostile Native Americans on the Western frontier. President Abraham Lincoln put Frémont in charge of the Army's Department of the West.

After the Civil War, Kit Carson left military life and became a rancher in present-day Colorado. He died at the age of 58 when a major blood vessel in his throat burst. He is remembered as one of America's most famous mountain men.

JOHN C. FRÉMONT AND KIT CARSON

In 1866, John C. Frémont bought the Pacific Railroad. Buying the railroad was a bad decision that cost Frémont his entire fortune. He failed to make the payments on the loan. A year later, the railroad was **repossessed** by the state of Missouri.

In 1878, John C. Frémont became the governor of the Arizona Territory. In 1887, after retiring from politics, he wrote his autobiography, *Memories of My Life*. Frémont died in 1890 of a stomach infection. He was buried in Sparkhill, New York. Though he had lost his entire fortune and died in poverty, John C. Frémont will always be remembered as the Great Pathfinder.

Making a Venn Diagram

![ornamental divider]

A Venn Diagram is a great tool to use when you want to create a graphic that shows how topics are different, yet alike at the same time. In a Venn Diagram, two or more large circles overlap in the middle. The differences between the chosen topics are written in the large outer areas of the circles. Things that the topics have in common are written where the circles overlap.

Look at the Venn Diagram below. There are two large circles that overlap to show how Mexico and the United States were different and alike in 1846. In the large areas of the circles, the differences between Mexico and the United States have been listed. The overlapping sections of the circles list the ways that Mexico and the United States were alike.

TOPIC: _____Mexico_____   TOPIC: _____The United States_____

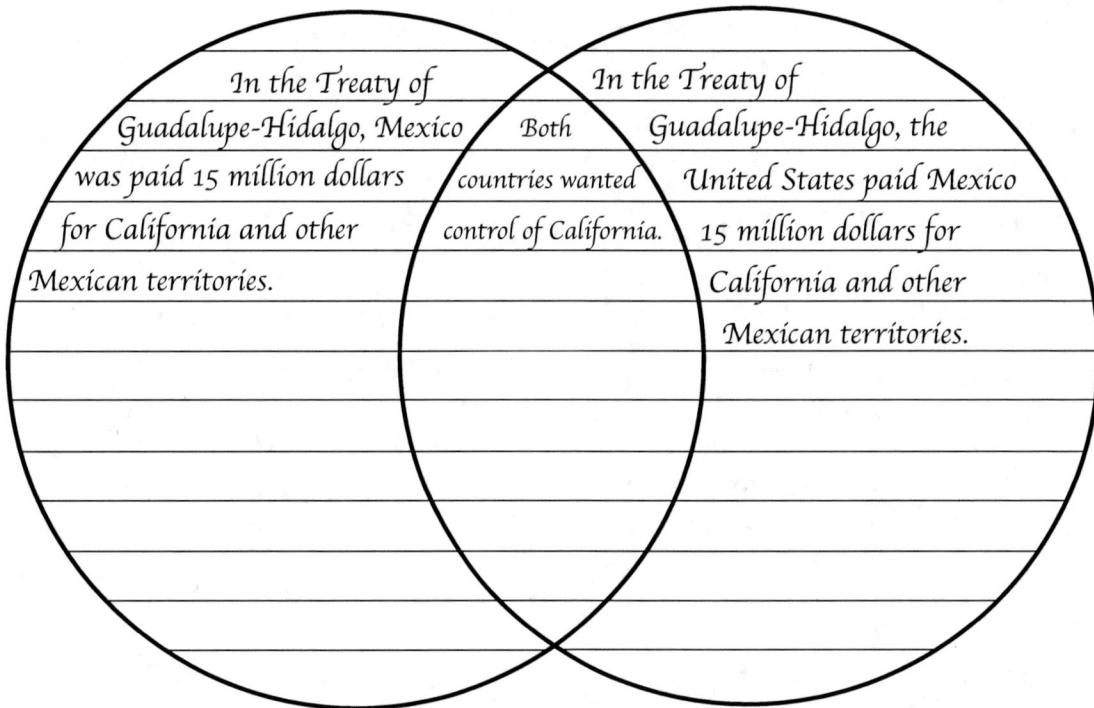

In the Treaty of Guadalupe-Hidalgo, Mexico was paid 15 million dollars for California and other Mexican territories.

Both countries wanted control of California.

In the Treaty of Guadalupe-Hidalgo, the United States paid Mexico 15 million dollars for California and other Mexican territories.

DIRECTIONS: In this activity, you will use the Venn Diagram on the next page to compare and **contrast** John C. Frémont and Christopher "Kit" Carson. Use the information you've read as well as other books, encyclopedias, and the Internet to find the information for your Venn Diagram. Follow the example by listing the differences between the two men in the large areas of the circles. Use the overlapping areas of the circles to list ways that John C. Frémont and Kit Carson were alike.

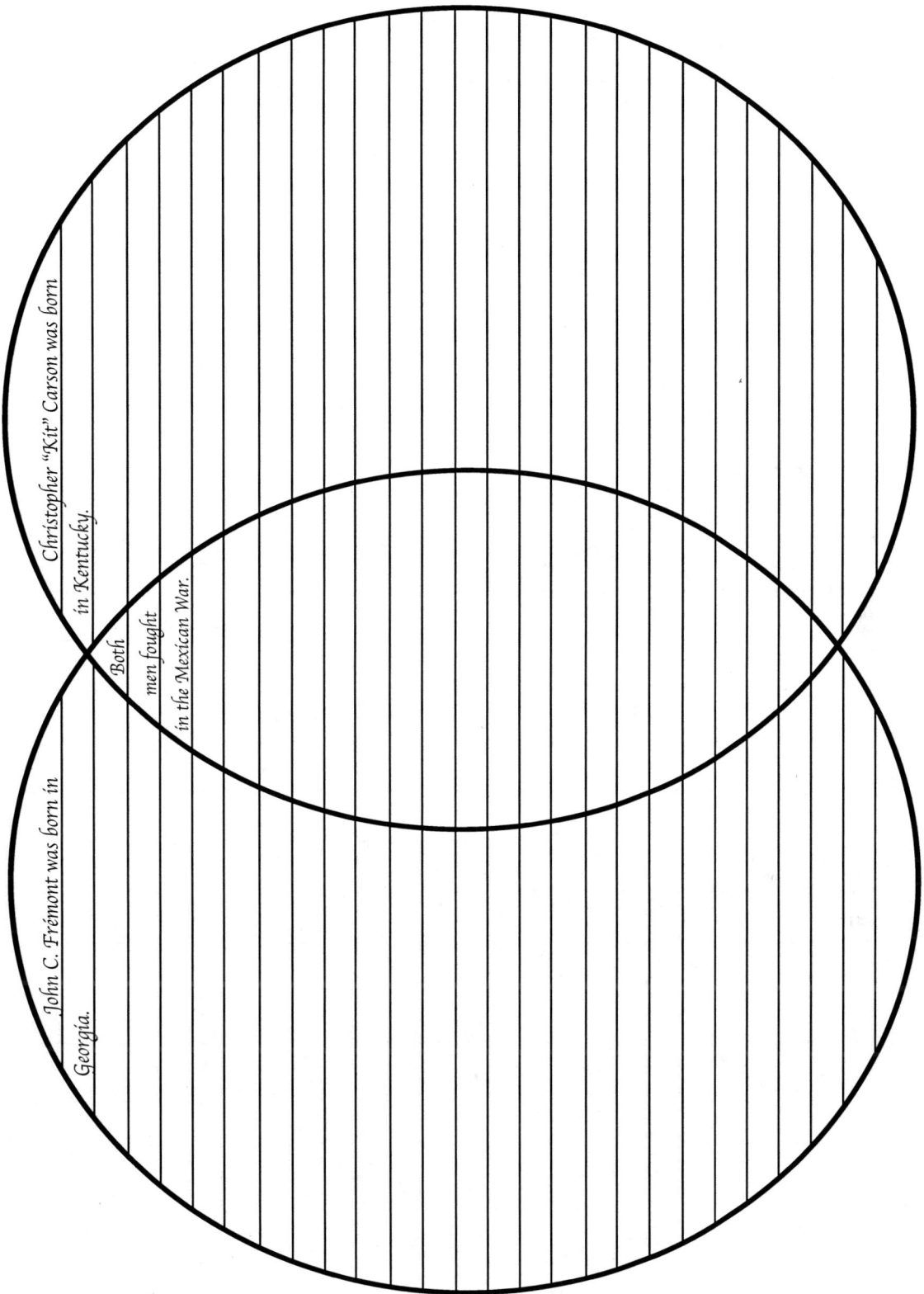

Name _____

TOPIC: _____ *Christopher "Kit" Carson*

TOPIC: _____ *John C. Frémont*

Christopher "Kit" Carson was born in Kentucky.

Both men fought in the Mexican War.

John C. Frémont was born in Georgia.

Westward Expansion © 2009
splashpublications.com

COMPARE & CONTRAST PARAGRAPH

DIRECTIONS: Use your Venn Diagram and a separate piece of paper to write a rough draft paragraph comparing and contrasting John C. Frémont and Kit Carson.

Your paragraph should include:

- a topic sentence clearly stating that you will be comparing and contrasting Frémont and Carson.
- two supporting sentences describing how the two were alike.
  Example: John C. Frémont and Christopher "Kit" Carson both fought in the Mexican War.
- two supporting sentences describing how the two men were different.
  Example: John C. Frémont was born in Georgia, while Kit Carson was born in Kentucky.
- a closing sentence that "sums up" your paragraph.

Have someone edit your rough draft paragraph before writing your final draft in the space below. Attach extra paper if you need more space.

☷☷☷☷☷☷ VOCABULARY QUIZ ☷☷☷☷☷☷
WESTWARD EXPANSION
PART VI

DIRECTIONS: Match the vocabulary word on the left with its definition on the right. Put the letter for the definition on the blank next to the vocabulary word it matches. Use each word and definition only once.

1. _____ outnumbered

2. _____ acquired

3. _____ Christianity

4. _____ outraged

5. _____ contrast

6. _____ devoted

7. _____ discrimination

8. _____ inland

9. _____ epidemic

10. _____ promoted

11. _____ raids

12. _____ exclusion

13. _____ rebelled

14. _____ founded

15. _____ republic

16. _____ resigned

17. _____ gristmill

A. the highest court in the state or nation.

B. people who are hired to perform household chores like cleaning, cooking, and caring for young children.

C. a disease that spreads quickly and affects many people at the same time.

D. a person who belongs to a religious group that was founded in 1830, and traces its beginnings to Joseph Smith.

E. moved up in rank.

F. established or set something up for the first time.

G. taken away because of failure to pay.

H. gained ownership of.

I. a member of the Senate, one of two groups of people elected to Congress to make laws for our country.

J. people sent to spread a religious faith.

K. types of rules designed to keep someone out.

L. a mountain range in eastern California whose highest peak in Mt. Whitney.

M. angered beyond belief.

N. battled against authority.

O. a business with big machines that saw wood into planks and boards.

P. toward the inside of a region; away from the water.

18. _____ legislature

19. _____ Supreme Court

20. _____ merchant

21. _____ missionaries

22. _____ estate

23. _____ repossessed

24. _____ senator

25. _____ Mormon

26. _____ superior

27. _____ reservation

28. _____ Union Army

29. _____ sawmill

30. _____ servants

31. _____ Sierra Nevada

32. _____ Continental Divide

33. _____ veteran

34. _____ basin

35. _____ formation

36. _____ Civil War

Q.   the line separating areas that drain into the Atlantic Ocean from those areas that drain into the Pacific Ocean. The line usually follows the tops of the Rocky Mountains.

R.   land set aside by the United States government for Native Americans.

S.   better than the rest.

T.   a low point in the Earth's surface that is surrounded by higher land.

U.   arrangement of something.

V.   a mill for grinding grain into flour.

W.   large country house on a big piece of land.

X.   having more people on one side than the other.

Y.   enters someone's property for the purpose of stealing.

Z.   a person who served in a military force or fought in a war.

AA. a group of people with the power to make laws.

BB. the war fought from 1861 to 1865 between the Union and the Confederacy over the issue of slavery.

CC. to show the differences.

DD. promised to be loyal to something.

EE. an independent nation with its own form of government, usually a president.

FF. buyer or seller whose goal is to make money.

GG. a religion based on the life and teachings of Jesus Christ.

HH. the Northern troops who fought against slavery during the Civil War.

II. treating some people better or worse than others without a good reason.

JJ. quit.

THE GOLD RUSH

In 1848, just a few months before the Treaty of Guadalupe-Hidalgo ended the Mexican War, something happened that would change the history of the United States forever. In California, John Sutter was having a sawmill built on his property. He hired a **carpenter** named James Marshall to be in charge of the **construction**. Mr. Marhsall and his crew were building the sawmill on the American River, near present-day Sacramento. It was there, in the muddy waters of the American River, that James Marshall found gold nuggets.

John Sutter tried to keep James Marshall's discovery quiet. He did not want people entering his property to search for gold. Within a few months, the secret was out. Most of Sutter's workers left him in search of their own fortunes. Sutter was unable to keep hundreds of **prospectors** from trampling his land, destroying his crops, and killing his cattle. People all around him were "striking it rich," but John Sutter lost everything and died a poor man.

THE FORTY NINERS

Within a year of James Marshall's discovery, thousands of people from the United States and other countries traveled to California to claim a piece of gold for themselves and hopefully become rich.

Gold-seekers from Australia, New Zealand, Hawaii, and China traveled across the ocean by boat. Prospectors from the United States and Mexico arrived on horseback and in covered wagons. Nearly 100,000 people traveled to California during that first year. Because the year was 1849, they became known as the "Forty Niners."

MINING FOR GOLD

In the beginning of the Gold Rush, miners "panned" for gold by scooping pans with screen bottoms into the muddy waters of California's rivers and streams. The holes in the screens were big enough to let sand fall through, but small enough to stop any flakes of gold large enough to have value.

Later, the miners used a method known as cradle rocking to search for gold. They scooped up the mud, sand, and water from the bottom of the river and dumped it into a box with a screen bottom. The miners rocked the box back and forth to separate the gold from the mud and sand.

After the gold in and around the streams had been removed, miners turned their attention to the land around the rivers. To remove the gold, hard-rock miners used picks and axes to dig **shafts** and tunnels that were up to 40 feet deep. Ox-drawn wagons carried supplies into the mines and gold out of the mines.

GOLD RUSH TOWNS

In 1848, before James Marshall's gold discovery, there were a few hundred people living in San Francisco. After gold was discovered, San Francisco became the starting place for most miners hoping to strike it rich during California's Gold Rush.

GOLD PROSPECTOR

Thousands of wagon trains packed the Oregon and California trails. Ships sailed across the Pacific Ocean. All were loaded with supplies and eager miners who started their golden journeys in San Francisco. By 1850, San Francisco's population had grown to 25,000.

From San Francisco, miners traveled to the towns of Sacramento or Stockton. These towns became the center of activity for prospectors heading to the northern and southern mines. After a long week panning for gold, miners returned to one of these towns for a hot meal, a warm bed, entertainment, and new supplies for the next week. Everything could be purchased with gold nuggets or bags of gold dust.

Gold Rush Mining Camps

After the first discovery along the American River, gold was discovered in the **tributaries** (TRIB•yoo•tair•reez) of the Sacramento and San Joaquin (wah•KEEN) rivers. Other gold discoveries were made around the Trinity, Klamath, and Salmon rivers. Temporary towns, or mining camps, were built near the mines. Gold miners lived in tents and wooden shacks where they survived on salt pork, biscuits, and molasses.

Hundreds of mining camps were created. In just a few short years, more than 465 million dollars worth of gold was mined in California. As these mining camps grew into towns, store owners with supplies were needed. Doctors, nurses, lawyers, ministers, and teachers soon arrived in California's new towns.

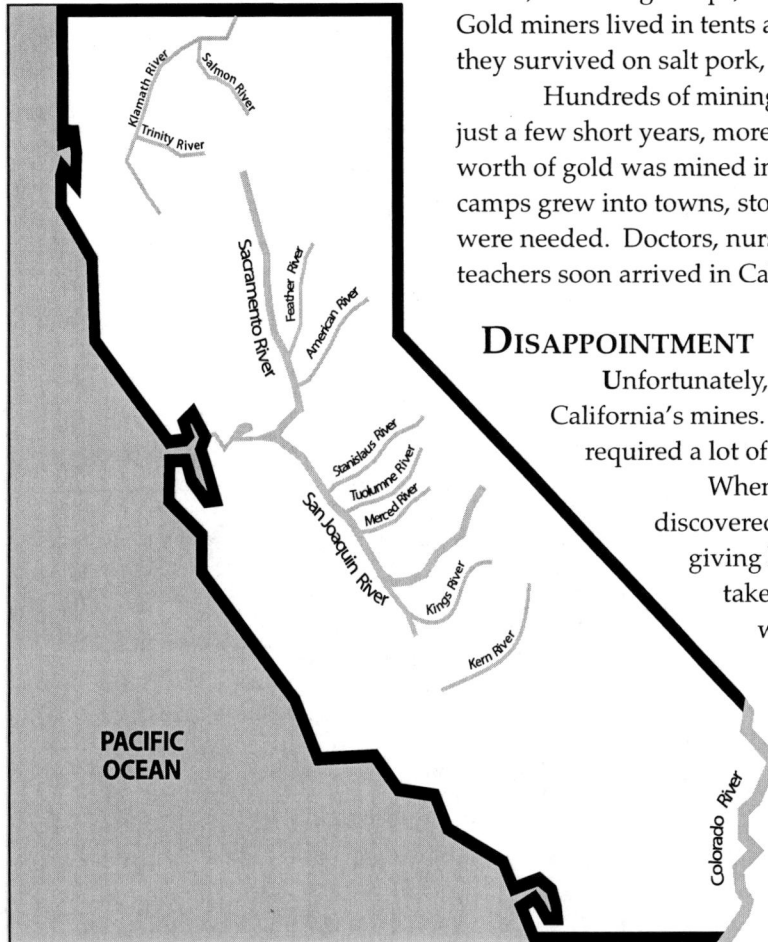

Disappointment

Unfortunately, not everyone found gold in California's mines. It was difficult work that required a lot of patience and money.

When a miner thought he had discovered gold, he filed a claim giving him the right to mine and take all of the gold he found. It was impossible to do all of the work by himself, so the claim holder hired miners to dig holes, lift large stones, and remove the gold.

Sometimes it took months or even years to actually find and remove the gold. During this time, the claim holder was responsible for paying his workers and supplying them with food, picks, shovels, pans, and mules. Most of the time, claim holders went broke before any gold was actually found and removed.

Other Gold Discoveries

California may have had the most famous gold discoveries, but it was not the only territory in the West experiencing a Gold Rush. Many disappointed miners left California when they heard the news that gold had been discovered in the Colorado Rockies, Montana, Oregon, New Mexico, Arizona, Nevada, and the Dakotas.

NATIVE AMERICAN CONFLICTS

Many of the gold discoveries were right in the middle of Native American territories that the United States government had promised would be protected from white settlement. The gold seekers didn't care about the government's rules or protected land. They trampled through Native American villages, hunting territories, and farms on their way to find gold.

Native Americans throughout the West fought back and tried to keep the white miners from entering their land. Because the Native Americans were not United States citizens, they had no rights. Bloody battles broke out. The United States Army was sent in to protect the miners and their families.

Sometimes a peace treaty was arranged between the Native Americans and the United States government. Most of the time, the Native Americans were forcefully removed from their land and sent to live on small reservations that were unfit for hunting, farming, or fishing. The United States government promised to give them food and shelter, but these promises were broken. The Native Americans lived in poverty. They watched helplessly as their **former** hunting grounds were destroyed.

OREGON COUNTRY

While the Gold Rush of California and other gold discoveries brought many settlers West, fertile farm land and wide open spaces in Oregon Country awaited families who wanted to settle and own a piece of land.

Remember, in 1818, the United States and Great Britain had signed a treaty that allowed people from both countries to trade and settle in Oregon Country. Thirty years later, thousands of American pioneers had made the dangerous journey across the Oregon Trail. As more American settlers entered the region, it was clear that the United States wanted Oregon Country for itself.

The United States and Great Britain did not want to go to war. Instead, in 1846, the two countries signed another treaty. In the agreement, Great Britain kept Vancouver Island and the land in the north that later became part of Canada. The United States took control of the land to the south. Both countries still claimed ownership of the San Juan Islands.

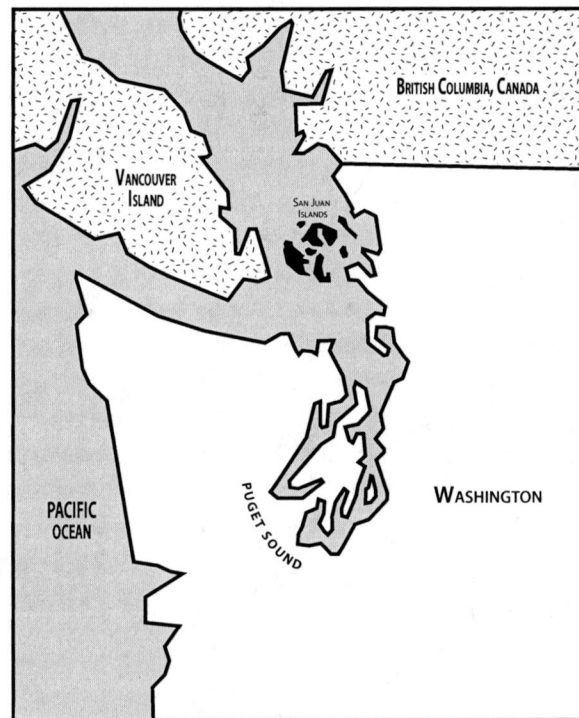

THE OREGON TERRITORY

In 1848, the United States created the Oregon Territory. This huge area of land would later become the states of Washington, Oregon, Idaho, and parts of Montana and Wyoming. By 1850, only 13,000 people lived in the Oregon Territory.

THE DONATION LAND ACT

In 1850, Congress passed the **Donation** Land Act. Congress hoped that giving away free land would encourage more people to settle in the Oregon Territory.

The Donation Land Act gave 320 acres of land to any white man who lived in the Oregon Territory before 1850. He simply needed to build a house and work on the land for four years. If the man was married, his wife was also given 320 acres of land.

White pioneers arriving from 1850 to 1855 were given 160 acres of land. An extra 160 acres was given to these men if they were married. Thousands of families poured into the Oregon Territory to claim their free land.

THE PIG WAR

You have already read that in 1846, the United States and Great Britain signed a treaty that divided Oregon Country between them. The agreement did not include the San Juan Islands. It was unclear which country legally controlled this small group of islands located south of the border between the United States and Canada. Both countries thought the islands should belong to them. American and English farmers and fur traders living on the islands had many disagreements.

PIONEER COUPLE

In 1859, an American farmer shot and killed a pig belonging to an English settler from the Hudson's Bay Company. The United States and Great Britain sent soldiers to the islands to keep peace. It was feared that killing a pig would finally send the United States and Great Britain to war over ownership of the San Juan Islands.

Instead of fighting, the United States and Great Britain asked Germany's ruler, William I, to decide which country owned the islands. After listening to both sides, William I decided that the United States had a stronger claim to the San Juan Islands. From that point on, the San Juan Islands became the property of the United States and the present-day state of Washington. Even though no shots were ever fired, the conflict was known as the Pig War.

THE HOMESTEAD ACT

In 1862, Congress encouraged settlement in the Nebraska and Kansas territories by passing the Homestead Act. The Homestead Act gave 160 acres of free farm land to any man who was at least 21 years old. He simply needed to agree to live and work on the land for at least five years. The Homestead Act granted more than 270 million acres of land to homesteaders.

THE GOLD RUSH

Directions: Read each question carefully. Darken the circle for the correct answer.

1 **Who discovered gold on John Sutter's property?**

   A John Sutter

   B Native Americans

   C Kit Carson

   D James Marshall

2 **Why were the gold seekers in California known as "Forty Niners?"**

   F It took them 49 days to travel to California.

   G The year was 1849.

   H There were only 49 people living in California before the Gold Rush started.

   J It took 49 years for prospectors to find gold.

3 **What kinds of tools did hard-rock miners need?**

   A Pans with screen bottoms.

   B Picks and axes.

   C Pans that rocked back and forth.

   D Trucks with very large tires.

4 **After reading about California's Gold Rush mining camps, you get the idea that –**

   F after gold was discovered, only a few hundred people traveled to California

   G gold was only discovered along the American River

   H gold mining did not offer comfortable living conditions or large amounts of food

   J less than one million dollars worth of gold was mined in California

5 **Which statement about California's gold miners is true?**

   A Most claim holders went broke before ever finding and removing any gold.

   B Mining for gold was easier than most people first thought.

   C Claim holders usually did all of the work themselves to remove gold from a mine.

   D Everyone found gold in California's mines.

6 **What happened to Native Americans during the Gold Rush?**

   F They became wealthy when gold was discovered on their land.

   G The government protected Native American lands from white miners.

   H The Native Americans were forced to sign treaties and give up their land.

   J The Native Americans helped the white miners find gold.

7 **What was the outcome of the Pig War?**

   A Great Britain took control of the San Juan Islands.

   B The Hudson's Bay Company took control of the San Juan Islands.

   C The United States and Great Britain agreed to continue sharing the San Juan Islands.

   D The United States took control of the San Juan Islands.

READING

Answers

1 (A) (B) (C) (D)   5 (A) (B) (C) (D)
2 (F) (G) (H) (J)   6 (F) (G) (H) (J)
3 (A) (B) (C) (D)   7 (A) (B) (C) (D)
4 (F) (G) (H) (J)

Famous People: George Custer and Sitting Bull

George Armstrong Custer was born on December 5, 1839, in New Rumley, Ohio. His father was a farmer and a **blacksmith**. As a child, George was sent to live with his half-sister in Michigan where he attended school. After graduating from high school, Custer became a teacher.

In 1861, Custer graduated last in his class from the United States Military Academy. Normally, someone who graduated last in his class would not become a high ranking officer in the military. George was lucky. The Civil War had just started and the Union Army was in need of officers. He became a second lieutenant and led battles against the **Confederate Army**. Lieutenant Custer was **admired** by other soldiers for his bravery and fearless leadership. He was even made a temporary general during the war.

After the Civil War, the United States Army reduced General Custer's rank to captain. Custer planned to earn back his military rank of general by helping the United States government with its battle against hostile Native Americans in the West.

Sitting Bull

Sitting Bull was born in 1831, near the Grand River in South Dakota. For the first year of his life in the Lakota Sioux (SOO) tribe, he was known as Jumping Badger. He received the name "Slow" because of his careful speech and ability to take food and objects without being caught. As a young boy, Slow loved to run and ride horses. He learned to shoot a bow and arrow and killed his first buffalo when he was just 10 years old.

GEORGE ARMSTRONG CUSTER

At the age of 14, Slow fought in his first battle against enemies of the Crow tribe. He knocked a Crow warrior from his horse. His father was so proud that he changed Slow's name to Sitting Bull.

Sitting Bull grew up to be a fearless leader who had the ability to communicate with animals and the spiritual world. He led his warriors in attacks against United States soldiers and white settlers who invaded Sioux hunting grounds and tried to push the Sioux from their land in the Dakotas. For his bravery and outstanding leadership abilities, Sitting Bull was chosen to be chief of the entire Sioux Nation.

THE FORT LARAMIE TREATY

In April 1868, the United States government and the Sioux Nation signed the Fort Laramie Treaty. Sitting Bull refused to sign the agreement, but other chiefs and their tribes agreed to end their war with the United States. In return, the Sioux Nation was permitted to keep about 240,000 square miles of its land. The United States government promised that the Sioux could remain on this land forever. White settlers would not be permitted to enter or settle on the Sioux Reservation.

Sitting Bull and many of his followers refused to move to the new reservation. For the next several years, they watched helplessly as white miners trampled through the Sioux territory and hunted buffalo for fun. The United States government made plans to lay railroad tracks right through Sitting Bull's former hunting grounds.

BROKEN PROMISES

In 1874, the United States government sent George Custer and a group of soldiers into the Black Hills of South Dakota. Custer was told to protect the railroad workers from Native American attacks. While in the Black Hills, Custer and his men discovered gold. The United States offered to buy the Black Hills for six million dollars. The Sioux Nation refused. They considered the Black Hills to be **sacred** and holy.

By the middle of 1875, thousands of prospectors had traveled to the Black Hills to seek their fortunes. They illegally set up camps right in the middle of the Sioux Reservation. Chief Sitting Bull and his warriors prepared to defend their land.

CHIEF SITTING BULL

The United States government made plans of its own. If the Sioux wouldn't sell the Black Hills of South Dakota, the United States was prepared to take it by force. The United States government opened the Black Hills for mining and warned the Sioux warriors to return peacefully to their reservation.

In early 1876, George Custer was sent to the Dakota Territory to force the Native Americans to return to their reservations. General H. Terry was in charge of the operation. In June, the group reached an area in the Montana Territory where they expected to find Sitting Bull and his Sioux tribe. General Terry ordered Custer's troops to travel ahead and position themselves south of the Native Americans.

SITTING BULL'S VISION

In the spring of 1876, Chief Sitting Bull gathered his warriors around him. He told the Native Americans that he saw a vision. The vision showed him that all of his enemies would be delivered into his hands. Chief Sitting Bull demanded that his warriors change their way of fighting. Instead of showing off to prove their bravery, the Sioux should fight to kill. If they didn't do this in the next battle, Sitting Bull believed that they would lose all of their land to the white settlers.

THE BATTLE OF LITTLE BIGHORN

On the morning of June 25, 1876, George Custer's men found a Native American village. The village was in the valley along the Little Bighorn River. Custer thought there were about 1,000 Native Americans in the village. He believed that his army of 650 soldiers could easily capture the small village. George Custer was mistaken. The Native American village actually contained at least 2,000 Sioux and Cheyenne warriors. They were led by powerful war chiefs Crazy Horse and Sitting Bull.

Instead of waiting for General Terry and his troops to arrive, George Custer decided to attack immediately. Custer divided his troops into three groups. Each group was sent in a different direction across the Little Bighorn River. Within two hours, Sitting Bull saw his vision come true. George Custer and his entire group of 210 soldiers had been killed. For the next 24 hours, the Sioux and Cheyenne fought Custer's other two groups.

General Terry and his troops arrived the next day. It was too late. The Native Americans had left the village. The Sioux and Cheyenne had been successful in the Battle of Little Bighorn. Still, the United States Army was stronger. Thousands of troops were sent to the area. By the end of 1876, the Native Americans had been forced to give up the Black Hills and move to smaller reservations within the Dakota Territory.

Sitting Bull and many of his followers escaped to Canada. In 1881, Sitting Bull returned to the United States. He was captured and thrown in prison. When he was released two years later, he moved to Standing Rock Reservation in South Dakota. He lived in a cabin on the Grand River, near the same place he had been born 50 years before.

CHIEF CRAZY HORSE

THE GHOST DANCE

A few years later, Sitting Bull started performing and teaching the Ghost Dance. The Ghost Dance was a special celebration that encouraged Native Americans to return to their native **customs** and religions. The celebration reminded them of a life free of hunger, disease, and constant fighting. The Native Americans believed that performing the Ghost Dance would cause the Great Spirit to return. The Great Spirit would raise the dead and destroy all white people in a flood.

The Ghost Dance frightened white settlers. They believed that the Native Americans were calling upon evil spirits to keep white families from settling on Native American land. The United States government **threatened** to attack if the Ghost Dance wasn't stopped.

Native American police officers were sent to arrest Sitting Bull. During the arrest, Sitting Bull, his son, and 12 others were killed. The great leader of the Sioux Nation was buried in present-day North Dakota.

FIND THE FIB

General George Custer and Chief Sitting Bull were two of history's most popular leaders.

In this activity, you will collect facts about General George Custer or Chief Sitting Bull to make a game called "Find the Fib."

DIRECTIONS:

1. Choose either George Custer or Chief Sitting Bull to make the game "Find the Fib."

2. Use your scissors to cut apart the George Custer or Sitting Bull "Find the Fib" cards given to you by your teacher. You will need 20 cards.

3. Neatly color the pictures of George Custer or Sitting Bull on each card.

4. Use the information about George Custer and Sitting Bull, encyclopedias, books in the library, and the Internet to find 15 true facts about the leader you have chosen.

5. Write each fact on a separate card. Try to fit the whole fact on one side of the card.

6. Make up 5 false facts, or "fibs" about George Custer or Sitting Bull. Make the fib as believable as possible so that it can't be easily seen as a fib.

7. Write each fib on a separate card, just like you did with the true facts. Again, try to fit the whole fib on one side of the card.

8. Mix and shuffle all of the cards together, so the true facts and fibs are mixed together.

9. Number the cards 1-20.

10. Make an answer key for yourself so you will know which cards are the true facts and which cards are the fibs.

11. Give your cards to 2 or 3 other people in the class to see if they can find the true facts and the fibs.

SAMPLE CARD

FRONT	BACK

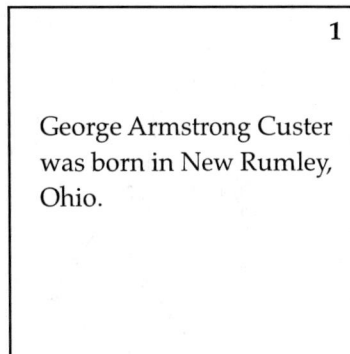

1

George Armstrong Custer was born in New Rumley, Ohio.

GEORGE CUSTER FIND THE FIB CARDS

SITTING BULL FIND THE FIB CARDS

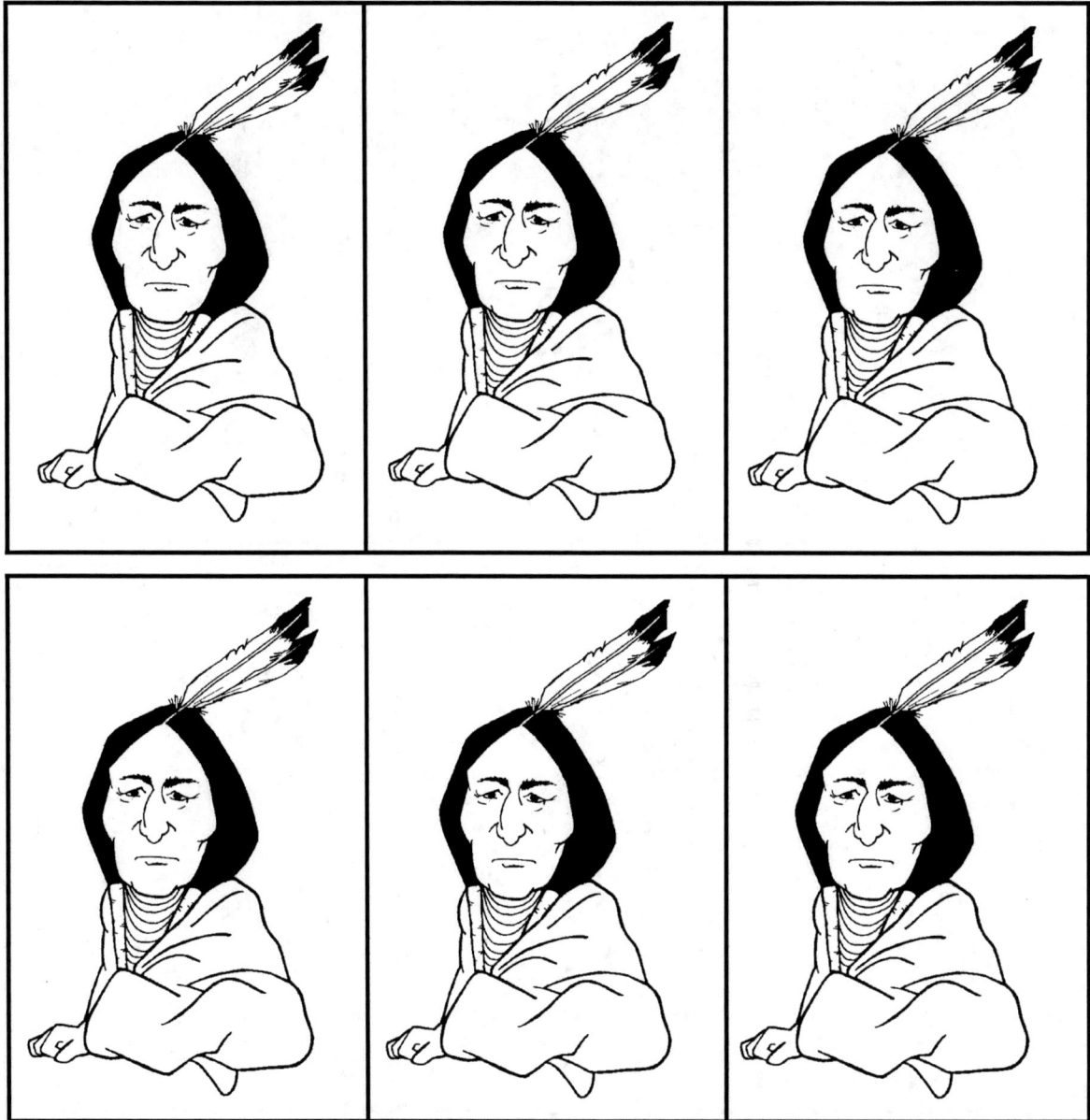

WESTWARD TRANSPORTATION

Getting from one place to another was difficult during our nation's early days. It took four to six months to travel to the West by covered wagon. Once people settled in towns, they walked or rode on horseback to get from place to place. Early settlers carried everything they owned on their backs.

STEAMBOAT TRAVEL

In 1787, **inventor** John Fitch made the first successful trial of a 45-foot **steamboat** on the Delaware River. Fitch later built a larger **vessel** that carried passengers and freight between Philadelphia and New Jersey. By 1796, Fitch had constructed four different steamboats, demonstrating that steam could be used to move boats through water.

After John Fitch's death, inventor Robert Fulton made history by building a steamboat that traveled from New York City to Albany. The 150-mile trip took 32 hours. By 1814, Robert Fulton and Edward Livingston were offering regular steamboat and freight service between Louisiana and Mississippi. Their boats traveled eight miles per hour downstream and three miles per hour upstream.

Beginning in 1852, steamboats traveled up and down the Colorado River, bringing supplies to miners in Colorado, Utah, Nevada, California, and Arizona. In the Pacific Northwest, steamboats were making regular trips from Oregon to Washington. The steamboats were faster than traveling on foot, but they could still only travel about 15 miles per day.

THE STAGECOACH

In 1857, one of the first types of **public transportation** was invented. It was a stagecoach. A stagecoach was a buggy pulled by a team of four horses that carried six to eight people over rough and dusty roads. Passengers sat on hard seats, usually surrounded by baggage and sacks of mail.

Not only was stagecoach travel uncomfortable, it was also dangerous. Accidents were frequent as the horse-drawn coaches traveled over steep mountains and narrow roads. There was also a good chance that the stagecoach would be robbed. Most of the time, stagecoaches were carrying passengers with valuables and mail sacks full of letters, some with money in them.

THE PONY EXPRESS

In 1860, William H. Russell, a businessman in California, put a plan into action to deliver mail from Missouri to California. Russell claimed that his Pony Express would complete the mail route in just 10 days. Operation of the Pony Express required 500 of the best horses and $100,000 in gold coins to buy all of the necessary supplies.

Only men who were under the age of 18, expert riders, and willing to risk death were invited to apply for the job that paid about $25.00 per week. Mounted on their swift horses, the "pony riders" raced with the mail from Missouri to California, a distance of almost 2,000 miles.

Although the Pony Express was successful in delivering the mail in 10 days, it was not a very profitable business. The horses could only travel about 10 miles per hour. Riders needed a fresh horse every 10 to 15 miles along the 2,000-mile journey. William Russell and his business partners lost about $200,000 during the 18 months that the Pony Express was in operation.

THE IMPORTANCE OF THE RAILROAD

The railroad played a very important role in the growth of the United States and Westward Expansion. In 1826, the first three miles of railroad tracks were laid in Massachusetts. The **Granite** Railway didn't carry passengers. It transported heavy granite stones from a **quarry** in Massachusetts to a dock on the Neponset River. A team of horses pulled the railroad cars along the track. The granite was loaded onto a boat and taken to Charleston, Massachusetts, where it was used to build the Bunker Hill **Monument**.

In 1827, the Baltimore and Ohio Railroad, known simply as the B & O, made plans to lay 350 miles of railroad track from Baltimore, Maryland, to the Ohio River in Virginia. Three years later, the B & O Railroad made its first scheduled run. Cars loaded with passengers were pulled by horses along 13 miles of track.

By the end of 1833, the South Carolina Railroad began offering passenger service from Charleston to Hamburg, South Carolina, on its steam-powered railroad. The cost for a one-way ticket was eight dollars. The train traveled up to 25 miles an hour, stopping every 90 minutes to reload with wood and water needed to power the steam engine. It took nine hours to make the 136-mile trip.

During the next 30 years, thousands of miles of railroad lines were laid throughout the eastern half of the United States. By 1852, passengers could board a train traveling from New York to Chicago and connect with other trains headed West toward the Ohio and Mississippi rivers. From there, steamboats transported passengers to places farther West.

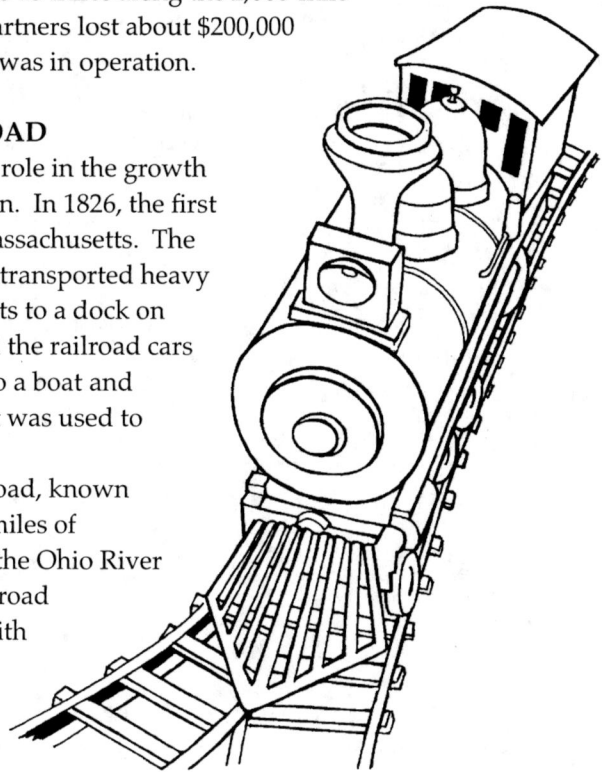

THE TRANSCONTINENTAL RAILROAD

In 1862, President Abraham Lincoln signed the Pacific Railroad Act. Work began on a railroad that would stretch from one end of the United States to the other. The Central Pacific Railroad laid 690 miles of track from Sacramento, California to Utah. The Union Pacific Railroad laid 1,087 miles of track from Council Bluffs, Iowa to Utah. Thousands of Chinese immigrants entered the United States to work for low paying jobs in dangerous conditions.

On May 10, 1869, in the city of Promontory, Utah, a golden spike was driven into the ground. The spike connected the Union and Central Pacific railroad tracks together. The **Transcontinental** Railroad connected the East and West by rail. A trip that once took six months now only took 15 days.

OTHER RAILROADS IN THE WEST

By 1883, the Northern Pacific Railway connected the northern section of the United States from St. Paul, Minnesota to Tacoma, Washington. That same year, the Southern Pacific Railway completed its 20-year project. The Southern Pacific stretched West from New Orleans, Louisiana to Sacramento, California, where it joined with the Central Pacific Railroad.

In 1893, the Great Northern Railway was completed. It ran through the Cascade Mountains, north of the Northern Pacific Railway. The Great Northern Railway connected the Pacific Northwest from St. Paul, Minnesota to Seattle, Washington.

Thousands of people headed West on the nation's new railroads. Ranchers used the railroads to transport herds of fattened cattle to the East. Timber and farm products were shipped all over the United States.

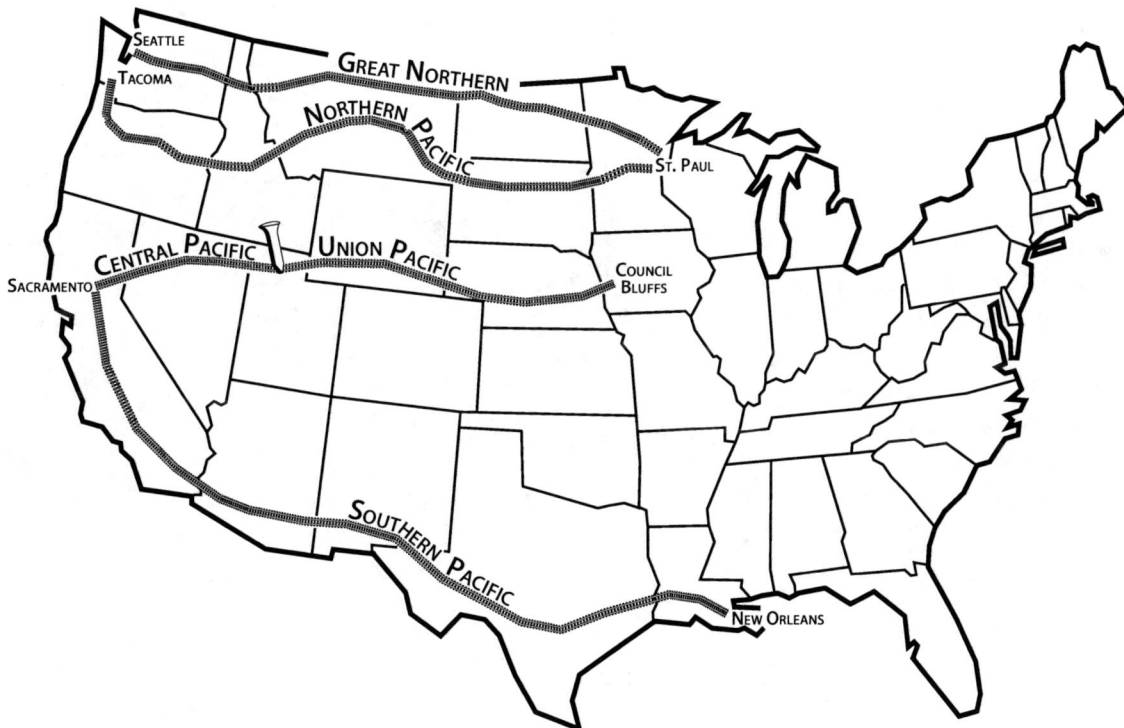

ROADS AND AUTOMOBILES

The invention of the automobile made getting from place to place even easier for those who could afford to own a car. Of course, roads that had been made for stagecoaches were not safe for cars. The first concrete roads were only 16 feet wide.

During the 1700s, the first steam-powered automobiles were invented. Like boats and trains, cars with steam engines burned fuel that heated water in a boiler. The steam expanded inside the engine and turned the wheels. Although steam engines were too heavy for cars, they continued to be successfully used in trains.

ELECTRIC CARS

In the 1800s, electric cars were invented in Scotland, Holland, and America. The first electric cars in America used batteries that powered small electric motors. Electric cars traveled up to 14 miles per hour. A fully charged battery could last for 18 miles before needing to stop and recharge. Electric cars were suitable for driving short distances, but by the early 1900s, better roads were built. People needed cars that could travel long distances from city to city.

THE MODEL T

In 1893, the first gasoline-powered automobiles were **manufactured** in the United States. By 1901, R.E. Olds was mass producing the Curved Dash Oldsmobile which sold for $650.00. A few years later, in 1908, Henry Ford began producing the Model T. The Model T was one of the most popular cars ever made.

The first Model T sold for $850.00 and used gas that cost just 20 cents a gallon.

Instead of starting them with a key the way cars are started today, cars like the Model T were started with a hand crank in the front that produced a spark and started the engine. Sometimes the engine would "kick back" before starting. The sudden reverse motion of the crank could break the starter's thumb or wrist.

THE MODEL T

The Model T's tank held 10 gallons of gasoline and traveled at speeds of up to 45 miles per hour. By 1918, half of all American car owners drove a Model T. Henry Ford told customers they could have the Model T in any color they wanted, as long as it was black.

AIRPLANE FLIGHT

For centuries, human beings have tried to fly like birds. People attached wings to their arms and jumped off high cliffs, flapping their arms as fast as they could. As most fell to their deaths, they realized that human arms do not work like birds' wings.

During the 1700s, people floated through the air in hot air balloons and **gliders**. Because these inventions depended upon wind to move, it was difficult to control their direction or speed. Inventors realized that power was needed to help humans fly.

In 1891, American scientist Samuel Langley built a plane that used a steam-powered engine. His model flew for almost a mile before running out of steam. Langley was given $50,000 to build a full size steam-powered plane. He was disappointed when he learned that his plane was too heavy to fly and crashed to the ground. Samuel Langley gave up his dream of trying to fly.

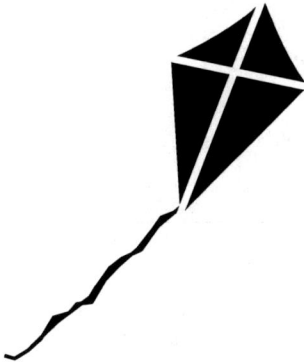

THE WRIGHT BROTHERS

In 1899, brothers Orville and Wilbur Wright began experimenting with unmanned gliders and kites to solve the problem of airplane flight. They watched birds and studied the works of inventors before them.

By 1900, the Wright Brothers had successfully tested their 50 pound glider, equipped with two sets of wings. They soon discovered that the wings did not have enough lifting power. The brothers set out to build a powered aircraft.

FAST FACTS

- In 1835, Samuel F.B. Morse and Alfred Vail invented the Morse Code **telegraph** system that sent messages over a one mile line of wire and then used a machine to print them on a piece of paper.
- The Morse Code communication system used dots, dashes, and spaces. Each letter of the alphabet was represented by dots, dashes, spaces, or a combination of all three.
- In 1841, the first telegraph was built between Maryland and Washington. Twenty years later, in 1861, Western Union built its first transcontinental telegraph line. The East and West were finally connected by telegraph.

THE FLYER

On December 17, 1903, Orville Wright completed the first manned airplane flight in history. While his brother Wilbur remained on the ground, Orville flew the 700 pound *Flyer* a distance of 120 feet. He was in the air for just 12 seconds. A year later, the *Flyer II* was flown by Wilbur Wright for more than five minutes.

In 1911, the Wright brothers designed the *Vin Fiz*, named after a grape soda. The *Vin Fiz* made the first successful flight across the United States. The flight took 84 days, stopping 70 times. It crash landed so many times that very few of its original parts were still on the plane when it landed in California.

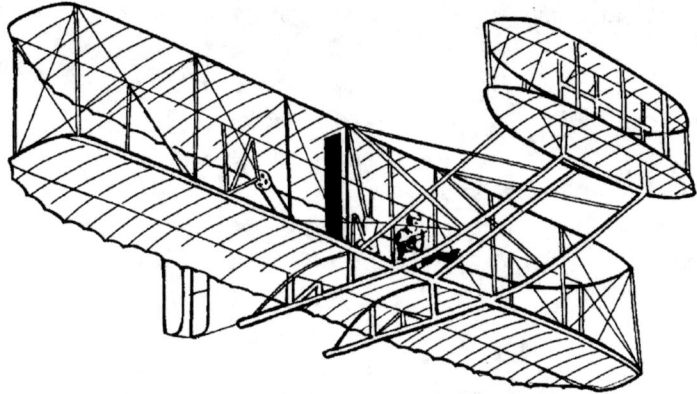

THE WRIGHT BROTHERS' *FLYER*

TODAY'S TRANSPORTATION

Today, people get from place to place in a variety of ways. Walking is still very popular and the cheapest way to get around. People ride bicycles, skateboards, and motor scooters for short distances.

Today's boats and trains carry more products than people, but it's still possible to cruise around the world's oceans in a ship or ride the rails from New York to California. Gone are the days of starting a black car with a crank. Today's automobiles start with the turn of a key or the push of a button. They come in all shapes, sizes, and colors. The United States has some of the best roads, highways, and bridges in the world.

Airplane travel has come a long way since the days of Wilbur and Orville Wright. There are more than 50,000 airports in the world ready to fly passengers any place they want to go. Today, a flight across the United States takes about seven hours, with no crash landings.

FAST FACTS

- In the 1850s, during the California Gold Rush, airplane trips across the Sierra Nevada Mountains were advertised. The advertisers planned to use steam-powered aircraft that could carry 100 passengers at speeds of 100 miles per hour. More than 200 brave treasure seekers eager to get to California as quickly as possible signed up for the trip. They were angry when they learned that no such steam-powered airplane existed.
- Before building and flying airplanes, the Wright brothers built and sold bicycles.
- The Wright Brothers National Monument is located in North Carolina, not far from where they made their historic first flight.

Name _____

🌀🌀🌀 WESTWARD TRANSPORTATION 🌀🌀🌀

Directions: Read each question carefully. Darken the circle for the correct answer.

1 About how long did it take to travel West during our nation's early days?

   A Two years

   B 15 days

   C Half a year

   D 24 hours

2 Which of the following statements about stagecoach travel is <u>true</u>?

   F Padded seats gave passengers a comfortable ride.

   G Stagecoaches were the safest way to travel during California's early days.

   H Stagecoaches were pulled by teams of four to six horses.

   J The one way trip from Missouri to California took just five days.

3 After reading about the Pony Express, you get the idea that –

   A it made William H. Russell a very wealthy man

   B the horses and supplies needed to operate the Pony Express were free as long as the mail was delivered on time

   C a Pony Express rider could use the same horse during the entire 2000-mile journey

   D if you were sixteen years old, you could be a Pony Express rider

4 The Transcontinental Railroad was finished in 1869. <u>Transcontinental</u> means –

   F across the state

   G across the continent

   H across the city

   J across the world

5 What was the problem with using steam engines in automobiles?

   A Steam engines were too heavy.

   B Steam engines used too much gasoline.

   C Steam engines used batteries.

   D Steam engines had to be started with a crank that could break someone's thumb or wrist.

6 Which statement about the telegraph system is <u>false</u>?

   F The telegraph system was invented by Samuel Morse and Alfred Vail.

   G The first telegraph was built between Maryland and Washington.

   H Telegraph messages were sent over a wire and then printed on paper.

   J In the Morse Code communication system, each letter of the alphabet was represented by a number.

7 Before building and flying airplanes, the Wright brothers built –

   A houses

   B bicycles

   C sawmills

   D cars

READING

Answers

1 Ⓐ Ⓑ Ⓒ Ⓓ   5 Ⓐ Ⓑ Ⓒ Ⓓ
2 Ⓕ Ⓖ Ⓗ Ⓙ   6 Ⓕ Ⓖ Ⓗ Ⓙ
3 Ⓐ Ⓑ Ⓒ Ⓓ   7 Ⓐ Ⓑ Ⓒ Ⓓ
4 Ⓕ Ⓖ Ⓗ Ⓙ

Making a Scale Map: The Pony Express

In 1860, the Pony Express successfully delivered the mail in 10 days. The journey stretched for almost 2,000 miles from Missouri to California. Riders required a fresh horse every 10 to 15 miles.

A map helps us track the movement of the Pony Express by giving us a small view of a big place. It would be impossible to show nearly 2,000 miles on a map that sits on your desk or fits on this piece of paper. Map makers use **scale rulers** to measure the long distances from place to place.

The **scale ruler** below can be used to measure the miles traveled by the Pony Express as the riders made their way to California. Each line on the ruler represents 10 miles traveled by the Pony Express. Every ten lines on the ruler equals 100 miles. The 100-mile lines on the ruler have been clearly labeled. Laying the ruler along the Pony Express route drawn on a map will show you long distances traveled without ever leaving your classroom!

Measuring using a Scale Ruler:

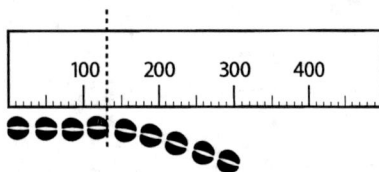

- Since the route is not perfectly straight, we will need to measure it in two parts.

- First, place the straightest part of the Pony Express route along the ruler as shown above.

- Make sure you line up the end of the ruler with the end of the horse hooves.

- Since we are measuring in miles, this part of the Pony Express route measures 130 miles.

THEN

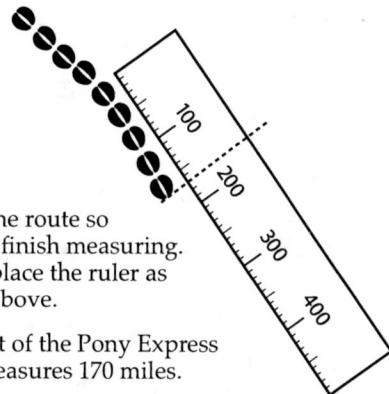

- Rotate the route so you can finish measuring. Again, place the ruler as shown above.

- This part of the Pony Express route measures 170 miles.

- Add both measurements to get the entire length of the Pony Express route.

- 130 miles + 170 miles equals 300 miles.

This part of the Pony Express route is 300 miles long! This is just one example of a **scale ruler**. The map maker decides the distance that will be represented on the ruler. On some maps, for example, each line on a ruler might represent 10 feet, 50 miles, or 1,000 kilometers.

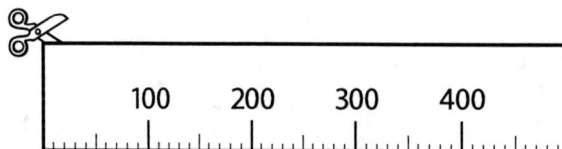

PART ONE

In the first part of this activity, you will measure distances using a **scale ruler**.

DIRECTIONS: Cut out the scale ruler from the first page. (Be careful when cutting out the ruler. Make sure you don't cut off the front of the ruler because this will affect your measurements.) Measure the distance in miles that the Pony Express riders traveled on their way to California. Kansas has been done for you.

MISSOURI

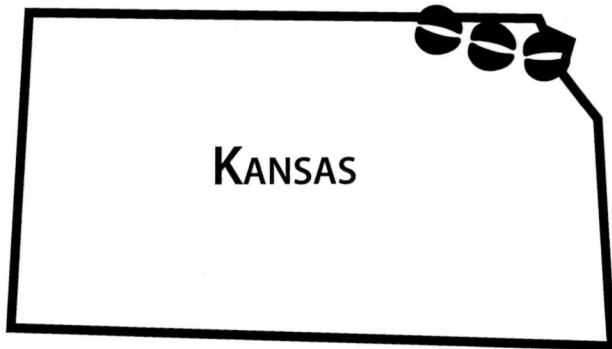

2. Using your scale ruler, measure the distance the Pony Express traveled through Missouri.

WORK SPACE:
ANSWER:

KANSAS

COLORADO

1. Using your scale ruler, measure the distance the Pony Express traveled through Kansas.

WORK SPACE:	120
	+ 50
	170
ANSWER:	170 miles

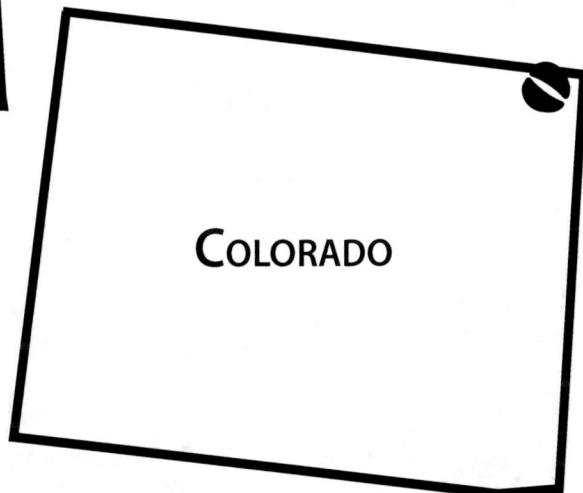

3. Using your scale ruler, measure the distance the Pony Express traveled through Colorado.

WORK SPACE:
ANSWER:

NEVADA

CALIFORNIA

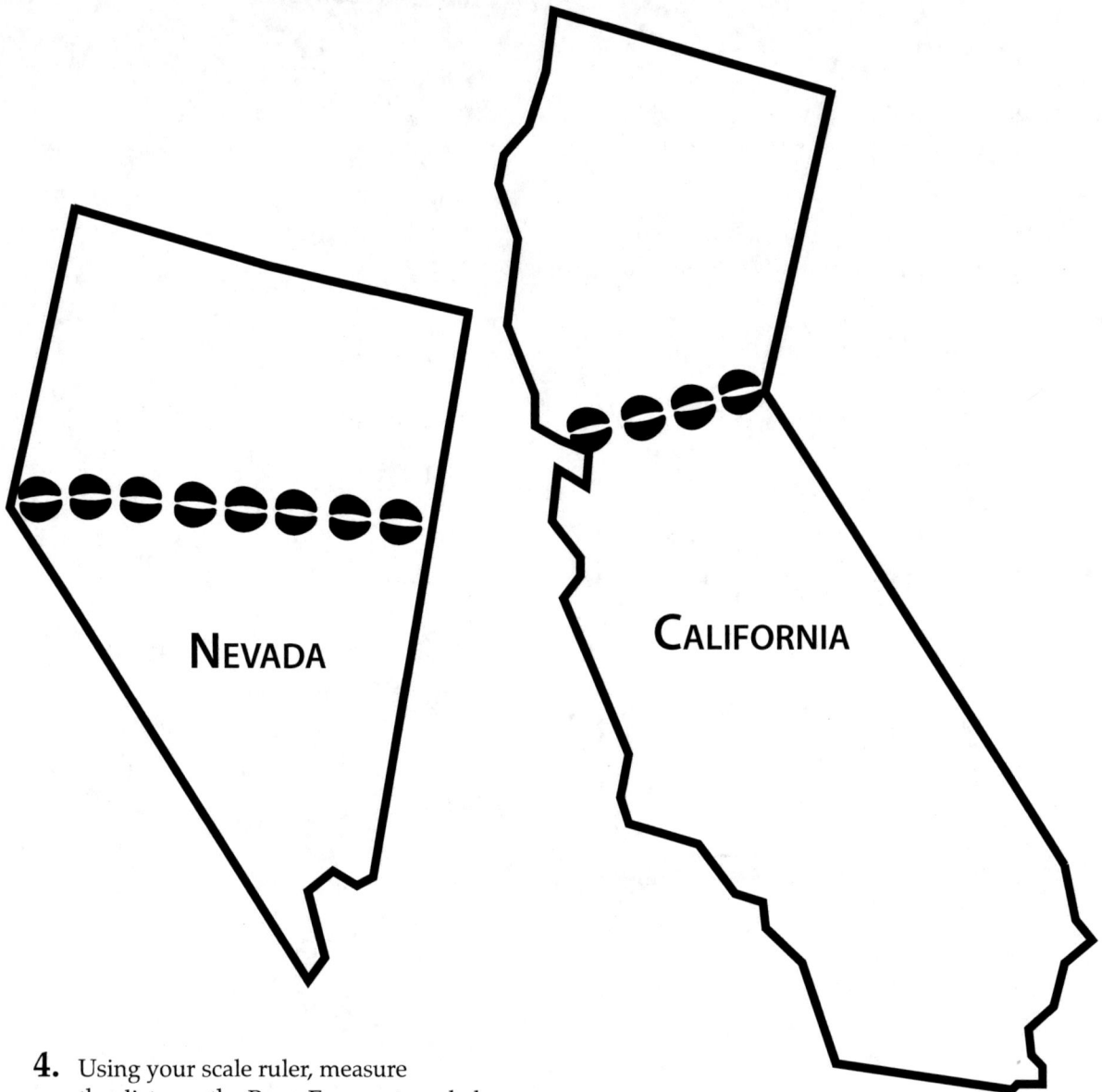

4. Using your scale ruler, measure the distance the Pony Express traveled through Nevada.

WORK SPACE:

ANSWER:

5. Using your scale ruler, measure the distance the Pony Express traveled through California.

WORK SPACE:

ANSWER:

NEBRASKA

WYOMING

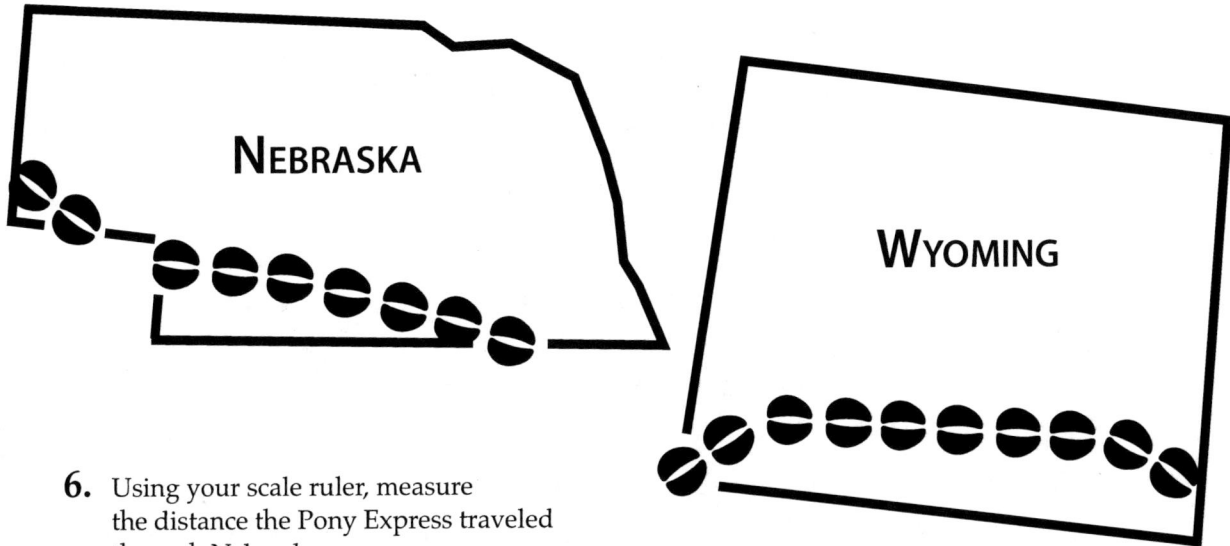

6. Using your scale ruler, measure the distance the Pony Express traveled through Nebraska.

WORK SPACE:
ANSWER:

7. Using your scale ruler, measure the distance the Pony Express traveled through Wyoming.

WORK SPACE:
ANSWER:

8. Add all of your answers together to find the **total** distance the Pony Express riders traveled from Missouri to California.

WORK SPACE:
ANSWER:

PART TWO: PUT IT ALL TOGETHER

In the second part of this activity, you will piece together the route traveled by the Pony Express.

DIRECTIONS: Cut out the scale maps below. Using a current map of the United States, arrange the maps in their proper order. When you are sure you have the maps in the correct order, glue them onto a separate piece of construction paper. Now you can clearly see the route traveled by the Pony Express riders from Missouri to California.

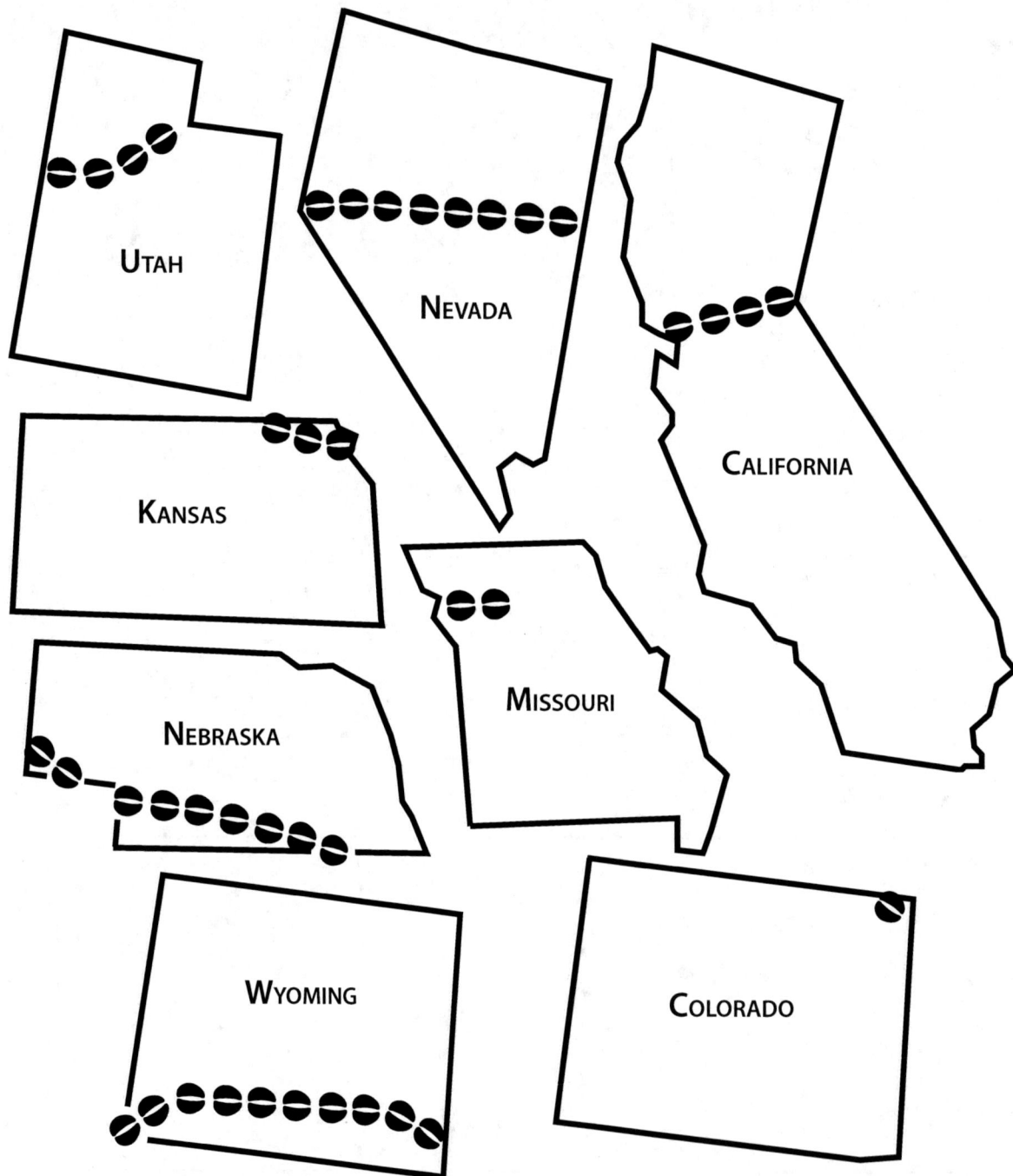

UTAH

NEVADA

CALIFORNIA

KANSAS

NEBRASKA

MISSOURI

WYOMING

COLORADO

◈◈◈◈◈◈ VOCABULARY QUIZ ◈◈◈◈◈◈
WESTWARD EXPANSION
PART VII

DIRECTIONS: Match the vocabulary word on the left with its definition on the right. Put the letter for the definition on the blank next to the vocabulary word it matches. Use each word and definition only once.

1. _____ admired

2. _____ transcontinental

3. _____ blacksmith

4. _____ telegraph

5. _____ steamboat

6. _____ quarry

7. _____ carpenter

8. _____ prospectors

9. _____ monument

10. _____ inventor

11. _____ construction

12. _____ manufactured

13. _____ shafts

14. _____ public transportation

A. people who explore areas for gold or other minerals.

B. well liked.

C. stretching across a continent.

D. long, narrow openings dug into the Earth.

E. building, stone, or statue created to remember a person or event.

F. work that involves putting something together.

G. large boat.

H. open pit that provides stones for building.

I. a boat that is powered by a steam engine.

J. light aircraft without engines that float through the air.

K. a system that moves groups of people from one place to another.

L. a machine used to send coded messages over a wire.

M. a craftsman who heats and hammers iron into different shapes.

15. _____ donation

16. _____ former

17. _____ customs

18. _____ Confederate Army

19. _____ threatened

20. _____ tributaries

21. _____ sacred

22. _____ vessel

23. _____ granite

24. _____ gliders

N. the Southern troops who fought to continue slavery during the Civil War.

O. someone who creates something new.

P. made something from raw materials by hand or machinery.

Q. a free gift given to someone in need.

R. streams that flow into larger bodies of water.

S. warned of danger or harm.

T. a craftsman who makes and repairs objects made of wood.

U. usual ways of doing things.

V. a hard rock formed millions of years ago that contains crystals.

W. coming from the past.

X. holy; not meant for human use.

Glossary

ac•quired gained ownership of.

ad•dict•ed not able to stop participating in harmful activities like drinking alcohol or using drugs.

ad•mired well liked.

a•do•be a heavy clay used for making bricks.

a•dop•ted accepted and put into action.

ad•vised helped make a decision and gave advice.

al•lies groups of people who come together to help one another in times of trouble.

am•mu•ni•tion bullets and explosive items used in war.

an•nu•al an event that takes place once a year.

ap•pen•dix a small pouch located at the upper end of the large intestine.

ap•point•ed chosen or selected.

ar•ti•facts objects and tools used by early humans for eating, cooking, and hunting.

A•sia the world's largest continent with more than half of the Earth's population.

as•tron•o•mer a scientist who studies the stars and planets.

at•tor•ney gen•er•al the highest law officer of the state.

au•to•bi•og•ra•phy the story of your life written by you.

ba•leen the bendable substance taken from the upper jaw of certain whales.

barbed sharp pointed hooks.

ba•sin a low point in the Earth's surface that is surrounded by higher land.

bi•og•ra•phies stories of a person's life written by someone else.

black•smith a craftsman who heats and hammers iron into different shapes.

bor•der lie right next to something.

bot•a•nist a scientist who studies plants.

bound•a•ries dividing lines.

ca•nine pointed, cone-shaped teeth.

cap•i•tal the city that serves as the center of government for the state or nation.

cap•tive a prisoner who has been taken by force without permission.

Ca•rib•be•an an arm of the Atlantic Ocean surrounded on the north and east by the West Indies, on the south by South America, and on the west by Central America.

car•pen•ter a craftsman who makes and repairs objects made of wood.

Cath•o•lic member of a Christian church who traces his or her history back to the twelve apostles.

cen•tu•ries periods of 100 years.

cer•e•mo•nies religious or spiritual gatherings.

Chris•ti•an•i•ty a religion based on the life and teachings of Jesus Christ.

chron•ic constant pain over a long period of time.

cir•cum•vent to go around.

cit•i•zens people in a city, town, state, or country who enjoy the freedom to vote and participate in government decisions.

Civ•il War the war fought from 1861 to 1865 between the Union and the Confederacy over the issue of slavery.

cli•mate the average condition of weather over a period of years.

coast an area of land that borders water.

col•o•nists people who are ruled by another country.

com•man•der a leader in charge of a military unit.

com•pan•ions people who travel together.

com•pe•ti•tion a battle for victory.

Con•fed•er•ate Ar•my the Southern troops who fought to continue slavery during the Civil War.

con•flict problem.

Con•gress the group of men and women in Washington, D. C. who are elected to make laws for the United States.

Con•sti•tu•tion the plan for the United States that outlines the duties of government and guarantees the rights of the people.

con•struc•tion work that involves putting something together.

Con•ti•nen•tal Ar•my American troops that fought against Great Britain during the Revolutionary War.

Con•ti•nen•tal Di•vide the line separating areas that drain into the Atlantic Ocean from those areas that drain into the Pacific Ocean. The line usually follows the tops of the Rocky Mountains.

con•trast to show the differences.

con•tri•bu•tions acts that involve giving money or time for a special cause.

con•ven•tion a meeting where important decisions are made.

con•vince talk someone into doing something your way.

cul•ture a group of people with a shared set of beliefs, goals, religious customs, attitudes, and social practices.

cur•rents quickly moving bodies of water.

cus•toms usual ways of doing things.

debt money that is owed to someone else.

de•feat•ed won victory over.

de•fend to keep safe from danger, attack, or harm.

del•e•gate a person sent with power to represent others.

de•scen•dants family members who come after one has died.

de•vot•ed promised to be loyal to something.

dis•crim•i•na•tion treating some people better or worse than others without a good reason.

dis•put•ed an area that two or more parties disagree about.

do•na•tion a free gift given to someone in need.

e•lect•ed selected by voting.

em•pire a group of territories or peoples under one ruler.

en•forced required someone to obey the rules.

En•gland a region located on the southern part of the island of Great Britain.

ep•i•dem•ic a disease that spreads quickly and affects many people at the same time.

es•cort•ed led away.

es•tate large country house on a big piece of land.

es•tu•ar•y lower part of a river that flows into the sea.

Eu•ro•pe•an a person who comes from the continent of Europe, the sixth smallest of Earth's seven continents.

ex•clu•sion types of rules designed to keep someone out.

ex•e•cu•tion carried out an order to kill someone.

ex•pan•sion the process of growing larger.

ex•pe•di•tion a journey for the purpose of exploring.

ex•port•ed sold goods to other countries.

fast•ed went long periods without eating.

fed•er•al government at the national level.

fer•tile rich soil that produces a large number of crops.

fi•nan•cial part of a business that has to do with money.

for•ma•tion arrangement of something.

for•mer coming from the past.

found•ed established or set something up for the first time.

fron•tier an area of land that has not yet been settled.

gen•er•os•i•ty giving freely of time or money.

glid•ers light aircraft without engines that float through the air.

gov•er•nor a person who is in charge of an area or group.

gran•ite a hard rock formed millions of years ago that contains crystals.

Great Bri•tain an island which includes England, Scotland, and Wales.

Great Lakes five large lakes located in North America at the border between Canada and the United States. The names of the lakes are Superior, Michigan, Huron, Erie, and Ontario.

Great Plains a grassland region stretching south from Canada to Texas where cattle are raised and wheat is grown.

grist•mill a mill for grinding grain into flour.

har•bor a sheltered area of water deep enough to provide ships a place to anchor.

har•poon a spear with hooks on it used for hunting whales and large fish.

harsh very uncomfortable conditions.

head•quar•ters main centers of operation.

head•wa•ters waters from which a river rises.

her•bi•vores animals that feed mainly on plants.

his•to•ri•ans people who study the past.

hos•tile very unfriendly.

il•le•gal•ly against the law.

im•mi•gra•ted permanently settled in another country.

in•ac•tive long periods with no movement.

in•de•pen•dence not under the control or rule of someone else.

in•fec•tious types of diseases that spread from one person or animal to another.

in•flu•ence having the power to affect others' actions and behaviors.

in•hab•it•ed lived or settled in a place.

in•land toward the inside of a region; away from the water.

in•ter•fere bother or disturb by giving advice when it isn't wanted.

in•ter•pret•er someone who turns one language into another language so people speaking different languages can understand each other.

in•vent•or someone who creates something new.

is•land area of land that is completely surrounded by water.

in•vad•ed entered an area and took it over by force.

keel•boat a shallow covered river boat that is usually rowed or towed and used for carrying supplies.

kid•napped took someone without permission.

leg•is•la•ture a group of people with the power to make laws.

loy•al faithful.

mam•mals warm-blooded animals that feed their young with milk, have backbones, and are covered with hair.

man•sion huge home.

man•u•fac•tured made something from raw materials by hand or machinery.

mer•chant buyer or seller whose goal is to make money.

mil•i•tar•y people who are part of the armed forces who may be asked to go to war.

mis•sion•ar•ies people sent to spread a religious faith.

mis•sions types of churches.

mon•u•ment building, stone, or statue created to remember a person or event.

Mor•mon a person who belongs to a religious group that was founded in 1830, and traces its beginnings to Joseph Smith.

moth•er coun•try a term used to describe the original homeland of the English colonists.

moun•tain•ous a place that has many mountains.

nav•i•gate control the direction of a ship.

ne•go•ti•ate discuss in order to settle something.

New World a term once used to describe the continents of North America and South America.

North A•mer•i•ca one of seven continents in the world. Bounded by Alaska on the northwest, Greenland on the northeast, Florida on the southeast, and Mexico on the southwest.

om•ni•vores animals that eat both meat and plants.

out•num•bered having more people on one side than the other.

out•raged angered beyond belief.

Pa•ci•fic North•west a region of the northwest United States that includes Washington, Oregon, Idaho, and Montana. It can also include the southwest part of British Columbia, Canada.

pelts skins and furs of animals.

pen•in•su•la a large piece of land surrounded by water on three sides.

pi•o•neers early settlers who prepared the way for others to follow.

plan•ta•tions very large farms in the South where crops of cotton and tobacco were grown and slave labor was usually used.

port city or town located next to water with an area for loading and unloading ships.

po•ver•ty extremely poor living conditions.

prai•rie wide area of flat or rolling grassland.

pred•a•tors animals that hunt and eat smaller, more helpless animals.

pre•served protected from injury or ruin so more can be learned.

prey to hunt another animal for food.

priests people with the authority to perform religious ceremonies.

pro•fit money made after all expenses have been paid.

pro•mot•ed moved up in rank.

pros•pec•tors people who explore areas for gold or other minerals.

prov•ince a part of a country having a government of its own.

pub•lic trans•por•ta•tion a system that moves groups of people from one place to another.

pur•suit desire to find.

Qua•kers members of a religious group that believed all men were created equal, refused to serve in the military, and would not pay taxes used to support war.

quar•ry open pit that provides stones for building.

raids enters someone's property for the purpose of stealing.

rat•i•fy to give legal approval by voting.

reb•elled battled against authority.

rec•og•ni•tion formal approval of an accomplishment.

reg•i•ment a military unit of ground troops.

re•pos•sessed something that has been taken away because of failure to pay.

re•pub•lic an independent nation with its own form of government, usually a president.

res•er•va•tion land set aside by the United States government for Native Americans.

re•signed quit.

re•sourc•es things found in nature that are valuable to humans.

re•treat to back away.

Rev•o•lu•tion•ar•y War battle for independence between the English colonists in America and Great Britain.

rit•u•al a ceremony performed the same way every time.

ru•mors things said in secret that may or may not be true.

sa•cred holy; not meant for human use.

saw•mill a business with big machines that saw wood into planks and boards.

sen•a•tor a member of the Senate, one of two groups of people elected to Congress to make laws for our country.

ser•vants people who are hired to perform household chores like cooking, cleaning, and caring for young children.

shafts long, narrow openings dug into the Earth.

shal•low a hole that is not very deep.

Si•er•ra Ne•vad•a a mountain range in eastern California whose highest peak in Mt. Whitney.

sib•lings brothers and sisters.

small•pox a dangerous disease which causes fever and bumps all over the skin.

steam•boat a boat that is powered by a steam engine.

su•pe•ri•or better than the rest.

Su•preme Court the highest court in the state or nation.

sur•plus an amount left over.

sur•ren•dered gave up.

sur•vey•or a person who does a detailed inspection.

tal•ons claws of birds.

tides rises and falls of the ocean.

tel•e•graph a machine used to send coded messages over a wire.

threat•ened warned of danger or harm.

tom•a•hawks axes that were used as tools or weapons by some Native American tribes.

tor•tured cruelly punished someone by causing severe pain.

trans•con•ti•nen•tal stretching across a continent.

trans•port to move products or people from one place to another.

trea•ty a formal agreement.

trib•u•tar•ies streams that flow into larger bodies of water.

tu•ber•cu•lo•sis a disease that attacks the lungs and causes fever.

ty•phoid fe•ver an illness that causes severe stomach cramps, bleeding, and sometimes even death.

Un•ion Ar•my the Northern troops who fought against slavery during the Civil War.

va•ri•e•ty many different kinds.

ves•sel large boat.

vet•er•an a person who served in a military force or fought in a war.

wa•ter•fowl birds that swim or live near water, like ducks and geese.

ANSWERS

ANSWERS TO COMPREHENSION QUESTIONS

THE NEW WORLD

READING
1. C
2. G
3. A
4. H
5. A
6. G
7. A

THE LOUISIANA PURCHASE

READING
1. A
2. H
3. C
4. F
5. B
6. H
7. A

THE LEWIS AND CLARK EXPEDITION

READING
1. A
2. H
3. D
4. G
5. B
6. H
7. C

THE SANTA FE TRAIL

READING
1. C
2. G
3. C
4. F
5. C
6. F
7. C

THE PACIFIC NORTHWEST

READING
1. D
2. H
3. D
4. H
5. D
6. G
7. C

THE TEXAS REVOLUTION

READING
1. A
2. G
3. C
4. G
5. B
6. J
7. B

THE OREGON TRAIL

READING
1. B
2. H
3. D
4. H
5. A
6. J

THE MEXICAN WAR

READING
1. D
2. H
3. C
4. F
5. B
6. J
7. A

THE GOLD RUSH

READING
1. D
2. G
3. B
4. H
5. A
6. H
7. D

WESTWARD TRANSPORTATION

READING
1. C
2. H
3. D
4. G
5. A
6. J
7. B

Answers to Famous People

FAMOUS PEOPLE:
ZEBULON MONTGOMERY PIKE

1. C
2. B
3. Answers will vary.
4. Answers will vary.
5. Answers will vary.

FAMOUS PEOPLE:
THE MAKAH

1. A
2. C
3. Answers will vary.
4. When a whale was spotted, the hunters jumped into their cedar canoes and paddled right up next to the huge animal. When the time was right, the chief hunter plunged his wooden harpoon into the whale's side. A long line of sealskin floats was tied to the other end of the harpoon. When the whale dove downward, the men tied on more lines with floats. As the whale grew tired, more men arrived in canoes to help kill the huge animal.
5. Answers will vary.

FAMOUS PEOPLE:
ANDREW JACKSON

1. D
2. B
3. Answers will vary.
4. Answers will vary.
5. Answers will vary.
6. Answers will vary.

FAMOUS PEOPLE:
DANIEL BOONE

1. A
2. A
3. Answers will vary.
4. Answers will vary.
5. Answers will vary.

FAMOUS PEOPLE:
ROBERT GRAY

1. B
2. D
3. Answers will vary.
4. Answers will vary.
5. Answers will vary.
6. Answers will vary.

FAMOUS PEOPLE:
GEORGE WASHINGTON BUSH

1. C
2. B
3. Answers will vary.
4. Fought in the War of 1812; wanted to raise his sons in a place that was free from discrimination; didn't take NO for an answer; became a successful farmer in Oregon Country; treated Native Americans with respect; was a friend to new pioneers who arrived on the Oregon Trail.
5. Answers will vary.

ANSWERS TO VOCABULARY QUIZZES

PART I	PART II	PART III	PART IV	PART V	PART VI	PART VII
1. D	1. O	1. K	1. X	1. N	1. X	1. B
2. G	2. U	2. W	2. F	2. JJ	2. H	2. C
3. Y	3. R	3. I	3. O	3. W	3. GG	3. M
4. Q	4. P	4. N	4. J	4. G	4. M	4. L
5. M	5. W	5. Q	5. D	5. EE	5. CC	5. I
6. B	6. F	6. M	6. G	6. M	6. DD	6. H
7. P	7. M	7. V	7. M	7. A	7. II	7. T
8. U	8. V	8. B	8. I	8. C	8. P	8. A
9. V	9. A	9. A	9. AA	9. R	9. C	9. E
10. R	10. L	10. L	10. C	10. FF	10. E	10. O
11. I	11. H	11. F	11. GG	11. E	11. Y	11. F
12. N	12. D	12. G	12. B	12. S	12. K	12. P
13. F	13. I	13. H	13. H	13. T	13. N	13. D
14. A	14. Q	14. P	14. L	14. P	14. F	14. K
15. X	15. C	15. C	15. CC	15. Z	15. EE	15. Q
16. J	16. J	16. D	16. FF	16. D	16. JJ	16. W
17. O	17. G	17. U	17. II	17. U	17. V	17. U
18. T	18. B	18. R	18. KK	18. O	18. AA	18. N
19. E	19. K	19. S	19. W	19. J	19. A	19. S
20. W	20. S	20. T	20. S	20. H	20. FF	20. R
21. L	21. E	21. J	21. N	21. K	21. J	21. X
22. C	22. N	22. O	22. Q	22. F	22. W	22. G
23. H	23. T	23. E	23. E	23. DD	23. G	23. V
24. K			24. Z	24. KK	24. I	24. J
25. S			25. K	25. BB	25. D	
			26. V	26. II	26. S	
			27. P	27. AA	27. R	
			28. A	28. V	28. HH	
			29. T	29. HH	29. O	
			30. EE	30. CC	30. B	
			31. R	31. X	31. L	
			32. U	32. GG	32. Q	
			33. DD	33. Y	33. Z	
			34. Y	34. B	34. T	
			25. HH	25. Q	35. U	
			36. JJ	36. I	36. BB	
			37. BB	37. L		

ANSWERS TO CONSIDER THE SOURCE

1. P	3. P	5. P
2. S	4. S	6. P
		7. P

LEWIS AND CLARK K•W•L•H GRADING CHART

CRITERIA	POINTS POSSIBLE	POINTS EARNED
Answering 2 Questions Before Beginning Research	**10** (5 points each)	
Completing 5 Sections of K-W-L-H Chart (What I **Know**, What I **Want** to Know, What I **Learned**, **How** I Found Out, **Sources** Used)	**80** (16 points each)	
Answering 2 Questions After Finishing Research	**10** (5 points each)	
TOTAL	**100**	

LEWIS AND CLARK PARAGRAPH GRADING CHARTS

CRITERIA	POINTS POSSIBLE	POINTS EARNED
Topic Sentence	**15**	
Four Supporting Sentences with appropriate information from Graphic Organizer	**60** (15 points per sentence)	
Closing Sentence	**15**	
Neatness of Final Draft	**10**	
TOTAL	**100**	

PARAGRAPH MECHANICS

CRITERIA	POINTS POSSIBLE	POINTS EARNED
Spelling	**20**	
Punctuation	**20**	
Grammar	**20**	
Capitalization	**20**	
Sentence Structure	**20**	
TOTAL	**100**	

ANSWERS TO PACIFIC NORTHWEST EXPERT'S JOURNAL

BLACK BEAR
Black Bears are large mammals in the Pacific Northwest. They are omnivores that usually roam the mountains and forests. Omnivores are <u>animals that eat both meat and plants</u>. Black bear cubs weigh about eight ounces at birth, but full grown females can weigh <u>600 pounds</u> and full grown males can weigh <u>1,200 pounds</u>. The fur colors of black bears can be <u>black, tan, brown, or yellow</u>.

BIGHORN SHEEP
The Pacific Northwest used to have a large population of bighorn sheep, but during the 1930s, the population was nearly destroyed by <u>over hunting and disease</u>. Male bighorn sheep are known as <u>rams</u>. Female bighorn sheep are known as <u>ewes</u>. Unlike most other types of sheep, bighorn sheep are covered with <u>an outer layer of brown hair instead of wool</u>. The underparts of bighorn sheep are <u>gray</u> and their tails are <u>white</u>.

MOUNTAIN LION
Mountain lions are the largest wildcats in the United States. They are also known as <u>cougars, pumas, or panthers</u>. In the Pacific Northwest, mountain lions can be found <u>in the forests and rocky areas where they can hide from predators</u>. They hunt for <u>mule deer, porcupines, and other small animals</u>. Predators of mountain lions include <u>bears, other mountain lions, and wolves</u>.

ELK
Elk are the deer-like herbivores. Herbivores are <u>animals that feed mainly on plants</u>. Elk can be easily spotted by <u>their large bodies and huge horns</u>. In the Pacific Northwest, elk can be found <u>in the high mountains and low valleys</u>. They eat mostly <u>grass and herbs</u>.

MOUNTAIN GOAT
Mountain goats live high up in steep rocky cliffs and ledges. Male mountain goats are known as <u>billies</u>. Females are known as <u>nannies</u> and baby mountain goats are known as <u>kids</u>. Mountain goats are known for their speed and ability to <u>climb steep cliffs quickly and easily</u>. Their hooves are <u>soft and curved</u> and act like <u>suction cups in rocky areas</u>.

CALIFORNIA SEA LION
California sea lions inhabit the Pacific waters from <u>Canada to Mexico</u>. They are members of the walking seal family and are known for <u>their intelligence, playfulness, and noisy barking</u>. Sea lions are preyed upon by <u>killer whales and great white sharks</u> but their main enemies are <u>fishing nets</u>.

RINGTAIL
Ringtails are small mammals weighing only two pounds. They are also known as <u>miners' cats</u> because <u>during the Gold Rush they were often found near mining camps</u>. Today, ringtails are located <u>near river valleys or springs where water can easily be found</u>. Their most striking features are their <u>tails</u> which are <u>as long as their grayish-brown bodies and striped with black and white rings</u>.

HARBOR SEAL
Harbor seals are found <u>on the Pacific Coast</u>. They split their time evenly between <u>land and water</u>. Harbor seals are true seals because <u>they have small flippers</u>. Harbor seals feed on <u>fish, squid, and small sharks</u>.

GREAT HORNED OWL
Great horned owls can be found throughout the Pacific Northwest. Great horned owls build their nests <u>high in trees</u>. They have also been known to steal the nests of <u>hawks, eagles, or crows</u>. Females lay <u>two or three grayish white eggs</u> that hatch in <u>about 30 days</u>. Young great horned owls are ready to leave their nests <u>60 days later</u>. Like most owls, great horned owls eat <u>small mammals</u>.

BALD EAGLE
Bald eagles can be found <u>throughout the Pacific Northwest</u>. They eat <u>fish, waterfowl, rodents, and rabbits</u>. Their nests can be <u>seven to eight feet across</u> and are usually built <u>in tall trees, high above the ground</u>. Female bald eagles lay <u>one to three eggs</u> that both parents take turns keeping warm for about <u>35 days</u>. Like great horned owls, bald eagles have wingspans that are <u>almost three times the lengths of their bodies</u>.

PEREGRINE FALCON
Peregrine falcons nest in the Pacific Northwest. They usually choose to build their nests <u>on cliffs and rock ledges that are close to water and prey</u>. Peregrine falcons hunt for <u>smaller birds and even eat bats that they are able to catch in mid-air</u>. In April, female peregrine falcons lay eggs that hatch in about <u>35 days</u>. Young peregrine falcons remain in the nest for <u>another 45 days</u> but stay close to their parents for <u>another four months after they are born</u>.

DOUBLE-CRESTED CORMORANT
Double-crested cormorants are commonly seen <u>nesting in the harbors on the Pacific Coast</u>. They choose these spots so they can <u>dive up to 25 feet below the water's surface in search of fish</u>. Both parents work together to build the nest. They also take turns <u>sitting on the eggs that hatch 25 days after being laid</u>. Baby double-crested cormorants wander from their nests <u>25 days later</u> to begin <u>finding their own food</u>.

MOUNTAIN CHICKADEE
Mountain chickadees can be spotted <u>in the Pacific Northwest just east of the Cascade Mountains</u>. Female mountain chickadees lay about <u>eight spotted or white eggs</u> in a fur-lined nest built <u>inside of a woodpecker hole</u>. The eggs hatch in about <u>14 days</u>. The young chickadees leave the nest <u>21 days later</u>. Mountain chickadees are constantly moving in search of <u>insects living in the forest's trees</u>.

YELLOW WARBLER
Yellow warblers are tiny birds with <u>greenish-yellow wings, tails, and legs</u>. Yellow warblers eat mostly <u>insects and fruit</u>. Yellow warblers choose to build nests of <u>grass, bark, plants, and fur</u>. Females lay <u>one to seven greenish-white eggs</u> that hatch in about <u>12 days</u>. Within two weeks, young yellow warblers are <u>ready to leave the nest</u>.

Expert's Journal Grading Chart

Criteria	Points Possible	Points Earned
Correctly Coloring 14 Mammals	**28** (2 points each)	
Two Interesting Facts about each Mammal	**42** (3 points each)	
Spelling/Grammar	**15**	
Neatness of Finished Book	**15**	
Total	**100**	

John C. Frémont/Kit Carson Paragraph Grading Chart

Criteria	Points Possible	Points Earned
Topic Sentence	**15**	
Four Supporting Sentences with appropriate information from Graphic Organizer	**60** (15 points per sentence)	
Closing Sentence	**15**	
Neatness of Final Draft	**10**	
Total	**100**	

Paragraph Mechanics Grading Chart

Criteria	Points Possible	Points Earned
Spelling	**20**	
Punctuation	**20**	
Grammar	**20**	
Capitalization	**20**	
Sentence Structure	**20**	
Total	**100**	

Find the Fib Grading Chart

CRITERIA	POINTS POSSIBLE	POINTS EARNED
Fifteen True Facts	**60** (4 pts. each)	
Five False Facts	**20** (4 pts. each)	
Spelling/Grammar	**10**	
Neatness	**5**	
Answer Sheet	**5**	
TOTAL	**100**	

ANSWERS TO PONY EXPRESS SCALE MAP PART I

1. 130 miles (+/- 10 miles)
2. 100 miles (+/- 10 miles)
3. 40 miles (+/- 10 miles)
4. 420 miles (+/- 10 miles)
5. 210 miles (+/- 10 miles)
6. 440 miles (+/- 10 miles)
7. 490 miles (+/- 10 miles)
8. 1,830 miles (+/- 70 miles)

ANSWERS TO PONY EXPRESS SCALE MAP PART II

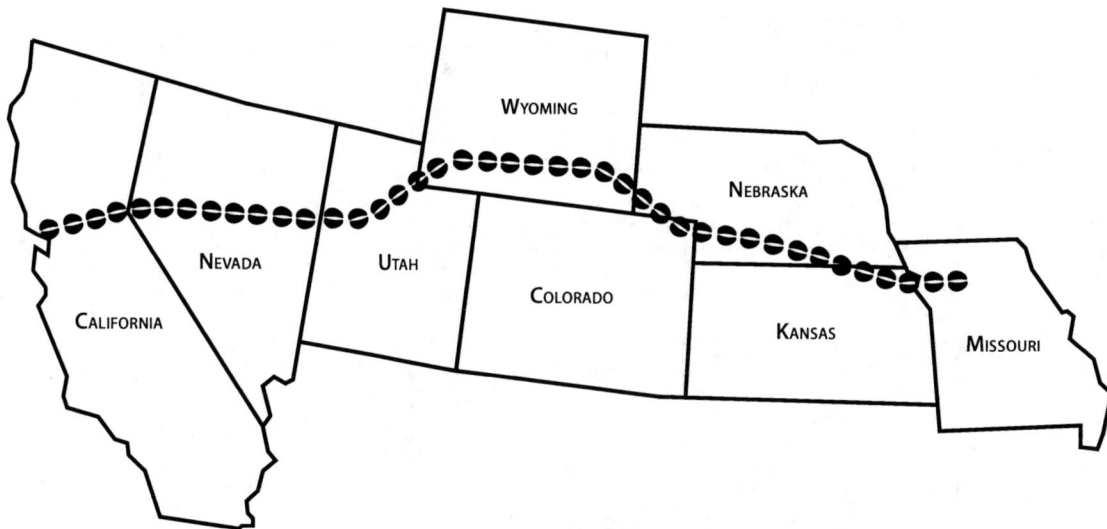

 # BIBLIOGRAPHY

Alter, Judy. (1998). *Santa Fe Trail.* Children's Press, New York.

Aylesworth, Thomas and Virginia. (1992). State Reports: The West. New York: Chelsea House Publishers.

Bellis, Mary: 'The History of Steamboats' 2008 [Online] Available <http://inventors.about.com/library/inventors/blsteamship.htm> (December 4, 2008)

Brusca, Frank: 'The Oregon Trail' 2002 [Online] Available <http://www.route40.net/history/oregon.shtml> (December 12, 2008)

Burke Museum of Natural History and Culture: 'Mammals of Washington' 2006 [Online] Available <http://www.washington.edu/burkemuseum/collections/mammalogy/mamwash/> (October 30, 2007)

Digital West Media: 'Desert Usa' 2007 [Online] Available <http://www.desertusa.com> (June 7, 2008)

Enchanted Learning: 'Lewis and Clark: American Explorers' 2007 [Online] Available <http://www.enchantedlearning.com/explorers/page/1/lewisandclark.shtml> (December 27, 2008)

Farcountry Press: 'Following the Voyage of Discovery: Lewis and Clark' 2007 [Online] Available <http://www.lewisandclark.com/index.html> (September 26, 2008)

Families First: 'Historic Trails of the Old West' 1997 [Online] Available <http://www.ida.net/users/lamar/trails.html> (November 6, 2008)

Gough, G.A, and Sauer, J.R.: 'Patuxent Bird Identification Infocenter' 1998 [Online] Available <http://www.mbr-pwrc.usgs.gov/id/framlst/infocenter.html> (July 22, 2008)

Great Northern Railway Historical Society: 'The Great Northern Railway' 2008 [Online] Available <http://www.gnrhs.org/index.htm> (January 24, 2009)

Hague, Harlan: 'The Search for a Southern Overland Route to California' 1976 [Online] Available<http://www.softadventure.net/roadcal.htm> (November 7, 2008)

Headley, Amy and Smith, Victoria. (2003). *Do American History!* Splash! Publications, Glendale, Arizona

Headley, Amy and Smith, Victoria. (2005). *Do California!* Splash! Publications, Glendale, Arizona.

Headley, Amy and Smith, Victoria. (2006). Do Texas! Glendale, Arizona: Splash! Publications.

Headley, Amy and Smith, Victoria. (2007). *Do Washington!* Splash! Publications, Glendale, Arizona.

HowStuffWorks, Inc.: 'Old Railroads' 1998-2008 [Online] Available <http://history.howstuffworks.com/american-history/old-railroads8.htm> (December 28, 2008)

HowStuffWorks, Inc.: 'Trail to Riches: The Gold Rush and Native Americans' 1998-2008 [Online] Available <http://videos.howstuffworks.com/hsw/12931-trail-to-riches-the-gold-rush-and-native-americans-video.htm> (December 28, 2008)

Illinois Historic Preservation Agency: 'Lewis and Clark State Historic Site' 2006 [Online] Available <http://www.campdubois.com/history.html> (October 29, 2008)

Lexico Publishing Group: 'Dictionary.com' 2008 [Online] Available <http://dictionary.reference.com/> (September 1, 2008)

Lindebald, Bengt: 'Westward Expansion' 2008 [Online] Available <http://www.americanwest.com/pages/wexpansi.htm> (November 4, 2008)

Makah Nation on Washington's Olympic Penninsula [Online] Available <http://www.northolympic.com/makah/> (November 25, 2008)

National Park Service: 'Fort Columbia State Park' 2006 [Online] Available <http://www.nps.gov/lewi/planyourvisit/fortcolumbia.htm> (December 8, 2008)

National Park Service: 'The Lewis and Clark Journey of Discovery' 2007 [Online] Available <http://www.nps.gov/archive/jeff/lewisclark2/circa1804/heritage/LouisianaPurchase/LouisianaPurchase.htm> (November 3, 2008)

National Park Service: 'Zebulon Pike: Hard-Luck Explorer or Successful Spy?' 2007 [Online] Available <http://www.nps.gov/archive/jeff/lewisclark2/Circa1804/WestwardExpansion/EarlyExplorers/ZebulonPike.htm> (November 3, 2008)

Oregon Historical Society: 'End of the Oregon Trail: Biographical Sketches of Black Pioneers and Settlers of the Pacific Northwest' 2008 [Online] Available <http://www.endoftheoregontrail.org/blakbios.html> (January 22, 2009)

Sierra Nevada Virtual Museum: 'First Airplane Flights Over the Sierra Nevada' 2008 [Online] Available <http://www.sierranevadavirtualmuseum.com/docs/galleries/history/transportation/firstflights.htm> (November 5, 2008)

Spartacus Educational: 'John Bidwell' 2004 [Online] Available <http://www.spartacus.schoolnet.co.uk/WWbidwell.htm> (February 4, 2009)

SunStar Media: 'Sea Otter Information' 1997 [Online] Available <http://www.seaotters.org/Otters/index.cfm?DocID=109> (January 2, 2009)

The Texas State Historical Association: 'The Handbook of Texas Online' 2003 [Online] Available <http://www.tsha.utexas.edu/handbook/online/index.html> (August 8, 2008)

Virtual Museum of the City of San Francisco: 'Pioneering Automobile Insurance' 1995 [Online] Available <http://www.sfmuseum.org/hist/autos.html> (October 4, 2008)

White, David: 'Social Studies for Kids: The Gold Rush' 2002 [Online] Available <http://www.socialstudiesforkids.com/wwww/us/goldrushdef.htm> (October 7, 2008)

Wright, Orville: 'How We Made the First Flight' [Online] Available <http://www.aero-web.org/history/wright/wriframe.htm> (December 3, 2008)